I have known Apostl[...]
operates in a duality [...]
humility are her platform. This book, *Pray Out Loud*, will not
only change your life—it will change nations.

—PROPHETESS ATAVIA BARNES
AUTHOR, *MISSING PIECES*

I have followed Apostle Kimberly Daniels for years, and my
life has been impacted by her ministry tremendously. She has
a unique way of demystifying the apostolic and prophetic.
Her teachings are sound and powerful. *Pray Out Loud* is necessary for this time we are living in. It will empower you to
pray with apostolic boldness and courage!

—SOPHIA RUFFIN
INTERNATIONAL SPEAKER AND AUTHOR,
SET FREE AND DELIVERED

God is equipping believers who will labor in intercession for
the release of God's power to win the lost, revive the church,
and impact society with the gospel of the kingdom. This is
not the time to cower in fear. We must stand up, speak up,
and pray out loud!

—MICHELLE MCCLAIN-WALTERS
AUTHOR, *LEGENDARY WOMAN*, *THE ESTHER ANOINTING*,
AND *THE DEBORAH ANOINTING*

PRAY OUT LOUD

KIMBERLY DANIELS

CHARISMA
HOUSE

Most Charisma Media products are available at special quantity discounts for bulk purchase for sales promotions, premiums, fundraising, and educational needs. For details, call us at (407) 333-0600 or visit our website at www.charismamedia.com.

PRAY OUT LOUD by Kimberly Daniels
Published by Charisma House, an imprint of Charisma Media
600 Rinehart Road, Lake Mary, Florida 32746

Copyright © 2021 by Kimberly Daniels
All rights reserved

Visit the author's website at www.kimdanielsministries.com.

Cataloging-in-Publication Data is on file with the Library of Congress.
International Standard Book Number: 978-1-62999-762-9
E-book ISBN: 978-1-62999-763-6

21 22 23 24 25 — 9 8 7 6 5 4 3 2 1
Printed in the United States of America

— ❧ —

This book is dedicated to my sister in the Lord, Toni Anderson of Crusaders Church in Chicago, and her beautiful family. Toni, you went into your prayer closet and entered into your rest in the presence of the Lord. I know you are resting in peace—RIP for real! I miss you, and I look forward to seeing you in glory when the last chapter of my book is written.

CONTENTS

FOREWORD

I HAVE BEEN THE apostle and covering for Kimberly Daniels for over twenty years. I have witnessed her dedication as she participated in my training, activation, and impartation gatherings. Kim has an unusual anointing as she operates in an undeniable gift of faith. When I first met her, I prophesied the Jael anointing over her life. Since then she has used the nail and the hammer to destroy strongmen in her community, the church, and the nations.

Recently I released a prophetic word over her life that "she is literally a wonder." I have seen miracles in the NFL, the political arena, the marketplace, and evangelism from her ministry.

Pray Out Loud will put an apostolic mandate on believers globally to open their mouths to decree, declare, and prophesy the word and the will of the Lord bodaciously.

God has blessed me to raise up and release spiritual sons and daughters to the nations. Kim is one of many who dare stand on the front lines for the kingdom to set their faces against the persecution of the modern-day church.

I cover Kimberly Daniels, and I agree with the saints at large to *pray out loud*! No longer shall our voices be muffled. There are many voices in the land, but the voices of the true believers will prevail and override the mockery and disrespect of the generation that hates God.

Let the shofar blow and the clarion sound of the apostolic and prophetic be released! The readers of the words in this book will release a sound that will shake wickedness out of the heavenlies and cause believers to pray prayers that will bring heaven down to earth.

Barriers of fear and intimidation will be penetrated as believers open their mouths and release the life and the death that are in the power of their tongues. Let the spiritual portals be opened and the breaker anointing come!

—APOSTLE JOHN ECKHARDT
CRUSADERS CHURCH
CHICAGO

INTRODUCTION

W E ARE LIVING in times of great discrimination against the message of the church. Special-interest groups boldly stand on platforms and speak out in ways that remind me of the times of David and Goliath. Goliath mocked the armies of the Lord, and the generals of that time hid and were afraid to speak out. God is recruiting voices from the wilderness of the America we live in today to stand and speak truth in love.

When I began writing this book, I was under major attack from antichrist groups on the internet. They demanded that I cease speaking about God on my personal Facebook page. It was difficult for me to believe this was happening in America, the country that had been dedicated to God. These anti-God folk wanted me to shut my mouth and be silent about my faith.

While I was in prayer about the situation, the Lord clearly spoke to me, saying, "Tell My people to not just laugh out loud (LOL) but pray out loud (POL)." God was not giving me another social media catchphrase; He was encouraging me to start a movement. That day at close to midnight, I issued a clarion prayer call. Over seventy thousand people logged on to my page. People were on fire for God! It takes only one match to start a forest fire.

As we prayed, God began to send me natural resources and allies in high places. Those prayer warriors and I took authority over the atmosphere and over Satanists and people from all arenas of the occult. Usually these social media critics continually troll you, but when God's people began to pray and speak

His Word into the atmosphere, their intercession took control over the powers of the air, and that stopped the warfare we were having on the ground.

Many are the afflictions of the righteous. We can't shut our mouths anymore. It seems every group is expressing itself loudly while the church is quiet. No more! As others are boldly proclaiming whatever they are passionate about, so should believers. This book calls believers to take a stand. "The people who know their God will be strong and take action" (Dan. 11:32, MEV). If we open our mouths and pray out loud, we can put the enemy to flight.

YOUR WORDS HAVE POWER

Throughout this book I will challenge you not just to pray but to pray out loud. That's because your words have power. By the words of almighty God creation was framed, and God placed that same creative force in your tongue.

Think about this: In Mark 4 a great storm arose while Jesus and His disciples were crossing the sea by boat. The storm was so powerful the disciples thought they were going to drown. All this time, Jesus was asleep, so the disciples woke Him up and said, "Teacher, do You not care that we are perishing?" The Bible says, "He rose and rebuked the wind, and said to the sea, 'Peace, be still!' Then the wind ceased and there was a great calm" (vv. 38–39, MEV).

The word translated "peace" in Mark 4:39 is *siōpaō*, and it means "muteness" or "inability to speak."[1] When Jesus rebuked the storm, He literally told the storm to shut its mouth. He was saying, "Hush now; be still and be muzzled." Notice also that the scripture doesn't say He rebuked His disciples. It says Jesus rebuked the wind and spoke to the sea. Jesus wasn't actually rebuking the elements—He was rebuking what was in the elements. He was dealing with the devil behind the storm.

That's what we have to do. As believers, we have the same power in our mouths to speak to every storm rising against the church and tell it to be still. We can speak things that are not as though they were (Rom. 4:17). The Bible says there is life and death in the power of the tongue (Prov. 18:21), so we need to use that God-given gift, because when we speak, all of heaven backs us up. We can no longer go around containing everything God has given us. If we don't use it, we'll lose it. It's time for us to open our mouths!

In Deuteronomy 1:8 God told the Israelites to possess the land. The word translated "possess" is *yāraš*, and it means "to occupy (by driving out previous tenants, and possessing in their place)."[2] This is what we're supposed to do to the enemy. We're supposed to displace him—to go in and take back the ground he has stolen. We do that by opening our mouths and proclaiming the word of the Lord out loud.

Today there is a loud minority and a quiet majority. There are more *for* us than *against* us, but we're not opening our mouths. All these agendas and special interests—it seems as if there are more of them because they're speaking more than we're speaking. The voice of God's anointed must be heard in the earth realm because our voices have more power than the voices of this world.

That's why throughout this book I have included prayers, declarations, and decrees. I want to equip you to open your mouth and pray for revival, peace, and justice. I've even included a passover deliverance prayer, a pandemic house blessing, and a prayer for frontline and essential workers in chapter 6, where we look at praying out loud for deliverance. I also want to help you get your spirit right before you pray, and I show you how to command the morning and pray so that your words hold weight in the spirit.

The Bible says God's people perish for a lack of knowledge. My prayer is that this book will equip you to receive impartation, change your life, and empower you to become a violent interrupter who stands in the gap with a loud voice to defend the gospel of Jesus Christ.

CHAPTER 1

PRAY OUT LOUD WITH HUMILITY

THE TRUTH OF God's Word is being challenged every day. Enemies of the gospel are building huge platforms and shouting their agendas with loud, demonic voices. Meanwhile the church is being pushed to the margins and held under the thumb of a vocal minority. There are more of us than there are of them, but our voices are being silenced. I'm here to prophesy, "No more!" God is calling us to open our mouths and not just speak out loud but pray out loud.

It's time to pray God's Word into the atmosphere. It's time to prophesy that His will be done on earth as it is in heaven. "Greater is he that is in [us], than he that is in the world" (1 John 4:4, KJV). It's time for us to proclaim that we will no longer be intimidated. If special interests can prophesy their antichrist agendas, we as believers can open our mouths and proclaim the good news. We cannot be ashamed of the gospel of Jesus Christ, "for it is the power of God for salvation to everyone who believes" (Rom. 1:16, MEV). We must cry aloud and spare not!

This book will give you the tools to declare the Word of God with boldness. But I warn you, humility is the covering this boldness must operate under. If we want to see lasting fruit and answers to our prayers, we must pray out loud in the right spirit with godly motives underlying our actions. That's why before we open our mouths to pray out loud, we must search ourselves.

THE SPIRIT OF NARCISSISM

This may be a peculiar way to begin a book about prayer, but I felt a strong pull in my spirit to address this topic. James 4:3 says, "You ask [God for something] and do not receive it, because you ask with wrong motives [out of selfishness or with an unrighteous agenda], so that [when you get what you want] you may spend it on your [hedonistic] desires" (AMP). God does not want us to be ignorant of the enemy's devices. When we pray and make the declarations laid out in this book, God wants us to be free of pride, selfishness, and the wounds of narcissistic abuse because this kind of bondage will hinder our prayers.

A lot of people talk about narcissism today, but it's more than a personality disorder. It is a spirit, and many don't realize how widespread it actually is because this spirit can be hard to identify. Many people have been wounded by narcissistic abuse; some have even been used by this demon—and they don't even know it. I operated for many years in relationships and even in ministry as a demon buster, and this spirit slipped through the crevices of my awareness.

The term *narcissist* refers to people who are extremely self-centered, have an exaggerated sense of self, and have unreasonable expectations of targeted individuals due to their deep-seated infatuation with themselves. The term is rooted in Greek mythology. Although myths are believed to be nothing more than folklore, I believe they often are related to spirits or gods that were worshipped in different cultures. For example, Zeus was actually worshipped by certain cultures in history. The Bible mentions the spirits of leviathan (the king of the children of pride), cockatrice (a mind-blinding spirit), and python (a spirit

2

of divination). If the Bible mentions these creatures, then they are not mythological but spiritual.

In Greek mythology, Narcissus was a young man known for his beauty. He was not handsome; he was beyond beautiful—so beautiful in fact that when he saw his reflection in the water, he fell in love with himself. He rejected all romantic advances because he felt no one could measure up to him. He stayed at the water, gazing at his own image, and eventually died of starvation because he refused to leave his reflection. According to the myth, a flower grew in the spot where he died, and today there is a flower called narcissus.[1] Why would so much attention be given to something that is only mythological? Does the story refer to a fictional young man, a flower, a personality disorder, or a spirit?

Let me be clear: a narcissist is not a person who is simply self-confident. Key words for defining *narcissism* are *excessive*, *apathetic*, *strategic*, and *endangering*. The manifestation of this spirit must be clearly separated from a person who has a lot of confidence. In Joshua 1:9 God commanded us to be strong and courageous. Everyone needs godly self-esteem, but the four key words I list draw the line between confidence and narcissism.

- **Excessive**—to operate in extreme measures that exceed the norm

- **Apathetic**—to have no care, empathy, or sympathy for things that one should be sorry for or sensitive to

- **Strategic**—to identify and target people, places, or things that fit the planned strategy of the narcissist

3

- **Endangering**—the targeted person is endangered or placed in a worse predicament after a narcissistic encounter of abuse

There are different kinds of narcissists, but the character traits or manifestations of people with the potential to engage in narcissistic abuse include

- a sense of entitlement
- unreasonable expectations
- a lack of empathy or compassion
- a pathologically lying spirit (even about dreams and spiritual things)
- demonic stories and over-the-top fantasies through which narratives are changed to create delusions
- a tendency to be overbearing, controlling, and manipulative
- a fraudulent double life
- a shady past
- a history of rejection
- a tendency to avoid taking responsibility (which manifests as misdirection and blame shifting)
- a spirit of usury undergirded by opportunism
- a fear of abandonment
- strong insecurity
- discomfort with the praise of others

4

- a warring spirit that divides and conquers
- a cocky and demanding personality
- power and trickery
- an inflated ego or sense of self-importance
- emotional outbursts (such as hanging up phones, slamming doors, and verbal and physical abuse)
- a preoccupation with past accomplishments
- emotional unavailability and sometimes emotional coldness
- an unusual superiority complex
- envy and jealousy
- difficulty admitting mistakes or taking criticism (When mistakes are admitted, it is only to gain access when it seems that a door is closed.)
- projection of their weaknesses onto others
- separating people unto themselves
- infidelity, a lack of commitment, and betrayal
- inflation of connections and influence.

If you feel uncomfortable after reading the previous list, it may be necessary for you to pray for self-deliverance from any participation in or contamination from narcissism. Narcissism is the spirit of this age. I realize that to say someone is a narcissist is a serious thing. It's important to understand that a person can have characteristics of narcissism without being a narcissist. You can engage in narcissistic behavior without being a narcissist.

5

My goal is to help you recognize the manifestations of this spirit and renounce them so you can pray out loud with a right spirit. I include prayers at the end of this chapter to break the power of this spirit in your life, but for now, take a moment to renounce any of the things previously mentioned that may relate to you. Simply place your hand on your belly, call out every characteristic from the previous list that you've noticed in your life, and renounce those things in the name of Jesus.

NARCISSIST MAGNETS

One of the big questions in this chapter is, Have you ever been a victim of narcissistic abuse? The easiest way to determine this is by taking the narcissist magnet test. Narcissist magnets are

- overly empathetic
- rescuers
- overly forgiving
- raised by narcissistic parents
- overly positive.

People who have these characteristics are drawn into narcissistic situations. This is very scary because most of the people I know in ministry have at least four of these five characteristics. For those who don't identify with those traits, following are some popular tactics that are red flags of narcissism.

Mirroring

This is a tactic used when a narcissist studies an individual's likes, dislikes, habits, and other tendencies to pretend to have all the same things in common. For example, the narcissist may research the targeted person's religious beliefs, political stance, family activity, or even likes or dislikes on social media to mirror that person. This results in the targeted person thinking there is commonality or divine agreement in the relationship or situation.

The narcissist's facade or false representation of who he or she is deceives the targeted person. He or she pretends to like everything the targeted person likes and to dislike what the person does not like. Mirroring is a diabolical deception that causes the targeted person to become like the narcissist and fall in love with an image of himself or herself. The spirit is transferred and reinforces the power of its assignment. In other words, if I am under a narcissistic mirroring attack, when I look at the narcissist, I see myself, and in falling in love with this individual, I am in essence falling in love with an image of myself.

Gaslighting

This is when a person uses psychological manipulation on targeted individuals through statements or acts that make them question their reality and eventually their sanity. Examples of gaslighting include

- pretending to forget things that actually happened to make the targeted person think he or she is crazy and

- trying to make it seem as if the targeted person exaggerates everything, thereby belittling the person and delegitimizing what he or she has to say. Examples of gaslighting statements are "You are not hungry—you just ate," "I'm not cheating

7

on you—you are paranoid," "I never said that—
your friends are idiots," and "I never said you
were up for the next promotion."

Love bombing

Upon first meeting them, most narcissists present themselves as charismatic, ambitious, disciplined, and fun to be with. They master love bombing (in courtship) through attention and affection that is given only as deadly bait. Once the love bomber has hooked the person, emotional unavailability manifests through devaluation, mistreatment, humiliation, impatience, and the silent treatment. Eventually the person who has been love bombed realizes they have fallen in love with a delusion. Love bombing happens so quickly the targeted person does not realize he or she has been torpedoed by strategic and skillful manipulation.

Narcissistic supply

This is the satisfaction the narcissist gets from having a person under his or her control and manipulation. It's like the high drug addicts experience. The supply is the reward of the scheme. For example, if a narcissist makes the targeted individual break down and cry, though the narcissist may mask it, the crying is euphoric to him or her.

THE POWER OF HUMILITY

As I said previously, God wants us to raise our voices and pray out loud, but He wants us to do so in a spirit of humility, completely free of narcissism. God does not just dislike pride; He "*resists* the proud, but gives grace to the humble" (1 Pet. 5:5–6,

MEV, emphasis added). The word translated "resist" in that passage means "to range in battle against."[2] We know that if God is for us, it doesn't matter who is against us, because we will win in the end (Rom. 8:31). But the flip side is true as well: if God is against us, it doesn't matter who is for us, because we will lose.

This is why Scripture warns us again and again to avoid selfishness and conceit.

> But understand this, that in the last days dangerous times [of great stress and trouble] will come [difficult days that will be hard to bear]. For people will be lovers of self [narcissistic, self-focused], lovers of money [impelled by greed], boastful, arrogant, revilers, disobedient to parents, ungrateful, unholy and profane, [and they will be] unloving [devoid of natural human affection, calloused and inhumane], irreconcilable, malicious gossips, devoid of self-control [intemperate, immoral], brutal, haters of good, traitors, reckless, conceited, lovers of [sensual] pleasure rather than lovers of God, holding to a form of [outward] godliness (religion), although they have denied its power [for their conduct nullifies their claim of faith]. Avoid such people and keep far away from them.
> —2 TIMOTHY 3:1–5, AMP

> I beseech you therefore, brethren, by the mercies of God, that you present your bodies a living sacrifice, holy, acceptable to God, which is your reasonable service. And do not be conformed to this world, but be transformed by the renewing of your mind, that you may prove what is that good and acceptable and perfect will of God. For I say, through the grace given to me, to everyone who is among you, not to think

9

of himself more highly than he ought to think, but to think soberly, as God has dealt to each one a measure of faith.

—ROMANS 12:1–3

Thus says the Lord: Let not the wise man glory in his wisdom, and let not the mighty man glory in his might, let not the rich man glory in his riches.

—JEREMIAH 9:23, MEV

To destroy the spiritual magnets that draw narcissistic people to us and cause us to be narcissists as well, we must walk in humility. There are two ways we can walk in humility: we can humble ourselves, or we can make God step in and humble us publicly. Luke 20:18 says, "Whoever falls on that stone will be broken. But he on whom it falls will be crushed to powder" (MEV). In other words, we must fall on the rock (Jesus) so we don't experience the humiliation of the rock falling on us.

If you believe you have experienced the ungodly fruits of narcissism, there is hope. Receive the healing balm of Gilead. Narcissism is just another spirit when compared with the power of God. "Greater is he that is in you, than he that is in the world" (1 John 4:4).

The flesh, the devil, and the world are full of selfishness. When we pray out loud, declaring God's Word to folk who hate and attack us, we must walk in Christ's love and humility. Pride and narcissism have no place in the kingdom of God and especially not in intercession. Take the time to search your heart, and use the following prayers as guides to shake yourself free of the influence of a spirit of narcissism so you can pray out loud with power.

LET'S PRAY OUT LOUD AGAINST
A NARCISSISTIC SPIRIT!

In the name of Jesus, I renounce every spirit of narcissism assigned against me personally, my children, my relatives, and my generation. I renounce every spirit released to make me fall in love with myself or to use me against people I associate with. I renounce the threefold cord of me, myself, and I. I present myself (my body) as a living sacrifice, holy and acceptable unto the Lord, which is my reasonable service.

I commit to being transformed into the image of God. I renounce obsession with my image or my reflection. I renounce being conformed to the ways of the world or what people think about me. I thank Jesus for the good, the acceptable, and the perfect will of God in my life. I will know the will of God for myself. I will not be thrown off course by delusion or false reflections and images. I renounce the spirit of magnification that would make me think more highly of myself than I ought to. I renounce every magnet that would draw narcissistic people into my life. (Name the magnets that apply to you.)

I renounce self-idolatry, and I confess that I refuse to be a lover of myself. I humble myself under the mighty hand of God, and I will wait for Him to exalt me in due season. I walk in humility, and I willingly lower myself to the floor in the spirit. I will fall on the rock, and the rock will not fall upon me. I receive godly humility so humiliation will not be my portion. In Jesus' name, amen.

Now place your hand on your belly and renounce the following traits.

I break the power of narcissism in my life. I decree and declare that I am not

- *self-absorbed*
- *self-admiring*
- *self-appointed*
- *self-assuming*
- *overly self-aware*
- *self-blinded*
- *self-centered*
- *self-collected*
- *self-conceited*
- *self-concerned*
- *self-conscious*
- *self-consumed*
- *self-deluded*
- *self-exalting*
- *self-flattering*
- *self-idolizing*
- *self-important*
- *selfish*
- *self-loving*
- *self-pitying*
- *self-pleasing*
- *self-preferring*
- *proud*
- *self-reverent*

- *self-righteous*
- *self-seeking*
- *self-willed*
- *self-worshipping*
- *self-seduced*
- *self-gratified*
- *self-made.*

Now raise your hands and praise God for setting you free!

LET'S PRAY OUT LOUD AGAINST A NARCISSISTIC ATTACK OR ASSIGNMENT!

Because magnets turned back-to-back will not connect, I turn every magnet that would draw narcissism into my life, by assignment or attack, back-to-back. I refuse to be victimized by narcissism. I have victory over every spirit that comes with this strongman. I will not be controlled by the spirit of entitlement, usury, lies, faultfinding, manipulation, retaliation due to abandonment and separation anxiety, trickery, grandiosity, power, and other spirits that come from inter-personality exploitative behavior. I send every attack of demonic mirroring, psychological gaslighting, and love bombing back through the gates of hell to the pit of its origination. Every narcissistic assignment against my profession, ministry, church, family, children, friendships, and relationships is broken in Jesus' name. I have an alarm in my spiritual discerner that will alert me when people who entertain and carry spirits of this nature come into my life. I draw a bloodline around myself and all that concerns me that the demon of narcissism cannot cross. In Jesus' name, amen.

LET'S PRAY OUT LOUD TO RELEASE A SPIRIT OF HUMILITY!

Lord, You said that You will dwell with him who has a contrite and humble spirit and that You will revive the spirit of the humble and the hearts of the contrite ones. Let me be as they are. You said that if I humble myself, pray, and seek Your face and turn from my wicked ways, You will hear from heaven and forgive my sin and heal my land. Lord, I will do as You have commanded (2 Chron. 7:14). I repent of pride now in the name of Jesus, and I humble myself in Your sight. I will not allow pride to enter my heart, in Jesus' name (Isa. 57:15). I take on the yoke of Christ, learning from Him, for He is meek and lowly in heart (Matt. 11:29). He humbled Himself and became obedient to the point of death, even the death of the cross (Phil. 2:8). I will not allow pride to enter my heart and cause me shame. I will be humble and clothed in wisdom (Prov. 11:2).

CHAPTER 2

PRAY OUT LOUD WITH A DISCIPLINED TONGUE

THE DAYS WE live in are evil, and as time goes on the days will only get darker. I'm not saying this to speak gloom and doom. The truth is, we can never deal with what is going on if we don't admit what is going on. The church has become a silent majority. Every special interest is getting louder about what's wrong while we're getting quieter about what's right.

The Scriptures call us to be watchmen on the wall. God told the prophet Isaiah, "Cry aloud, spare not, lift up thy voice like a trumpet, and shew my people their transgression, and the house of Jacob their sins" (58:1, KJV). That is the same message He is sending to the church today. Now more than ever we need to push past the boundaries of religious traditions, political opinions, and even the insecurities of our own hearts and pray out loud.

The Bible warns against those who see danger coming and don't say anything.

> But if the watchman sees the sword coming and does not blow the trumpet and the people are not warned, and the sword comes and takes any person from among them, he is taken away in his iniquity; but his blood I will require at the watchman's hand. So you, son of man: I have made you a

watchman for the house of Israel; therefore you shall hear a
word from My mouth and warn them from Me.

—EZEKIEL 33:6–7

In the Book of Isaiah, God likened these watchmen to "dumb
dogs, unable to bark; sleepers lying down, who love to slumber"
(56:10, MEV). There are many types of prayer—devotional prayer,
silent prayer, and relational prayer in our prayer closets. In this
season, God is calling us to be intercessors who cry aloud and
spare not—who boldly pray for the will of God to be done on
earth as it is in heaven.

But as we open our mouths to pray, we must be careful of
speaking out and saying nothing—just making a lot of noise. We
must pray in such a way that our words hold weight in the spirit.

The apostle Paul wrote:

> If I speak with the tongues of men and of angels, but have
> not love [for others growing out of God's love for me], then I
> have become only a noisy gong or a clanging cymbal [just an
> annoying distraction].

—1 CORINTHIANS 13:1, AMP

In order for our prayers to hold weight in the spirit, they
must be rooted and grounded in love. Ephesians 3:17–19 says
"that you, being rooted and grounded in love, may be able to
comprehend with all saints what is the breadth and length and
depth and height, and to know the love of Christ which surpasses knowledge; that you may be filled with all the fullness of
God" (MEV). Love is the foundation, the glue that keeps everything together, the door that takes our prayers to the next level.

Many people don't walk in love because they don't know

what love really is. The world cries, "What's love got to do with it?" The church should cry, "Love has everything to do with all things because God is love!" It is all about the *agape* love of God. Unlike English, Greek contains several words that are translated "love." The Greek word *agapē* refers not to brotherly or sensual love but to love that is from God. Because God is love (1 John 4:8), there is no higher love than *agape*.

Agape is the love that opens doors of knowledge and understanding. People who think they're smart are educated fools without the love of God. This is nothing to debate. A man who says there is no God is identified in Psalm 14:1 as a fool; it doesn't matter how educated he is. I realize I am probably offending some people at this point, and that is my absolute intent.

I'm taking the readers of this book to the water to see how many will lap like a dog, as the soldiers whom God had chosen to be part of Gideon's army did (Judg. 7:4–7). This message is meant to offend some to elevate others. Motives mean everything to God, and love is the motor that makes our lives run well. Love covers a multitude of sins and roots the fruit of having a disciplined tongue. Out of the abundance of the heart the mouth speaks; this means having goodness in the heart will affect our words.

Having a disciplined tongue and being a good steward of our words will launch us into new levels of victory in spiritual warfare. As I said previously, life and death are in the power of the tongue. This is the season when the church must speak life— out loud! We have murmured and complained under our breath about the opposition we face as believers, but just as it was with the children of Israel, so too if we continue in this posture, we will not enter into what God has for us. But before we deal with

17

murmuring and complaining, we need to understand the danger of speaking idle words.

SPEAKING IDLE WORDS

First Corinthians 13:1 says if we speak without love, we become like sounding brass or a clanging cymbal. A sound that is noisy and clanging is distracting. A distraction prevents concentration or diverts attention from what really needs to be focused on. Man or woman of God, what noisy, clanging things have been distracting you from what God wants you to be attentive to?

I once had a vision in which I saw individuals, ministries, churches, and various organizations that were on the front lines for the kingdom. They were represented as vehicles that appeared to be parked at stop signs (representing things that promote total failure) and yield signs (representing things that slow progress). I could hear their engines running, but the cars were not moving. I knew in the vision that the vehicles were in good shape and full of gas, but for some reason they were not moving. Then I saw the words *lull* and *idle*.

Let me be clear: God is doing some great and awesome things in the church. But in this vision, God was showing me that many individuals and ministries are stuck. They're not moving forward because God manifests His will on the earth through faith. I want to keep this simple so no one misses my point. We activate the visions God has given us through faith, and faith comes by hearing, and hearing comes by the Word of God (Rom. 10:17). We must get back to the basics of studying the Word of God, praying the Scriptures, and seeking the face of God so we can move forward in our assignments. Being idle with your words will cause you to get stuck.

I'm not saying the church has been out of God's will and is totally undisciplined. I am saying that the enemies of the gospel in our culture appear to be willing to make more sacrifices for their agendas. I am saying that what has been can be no more. Our spiritual warfare strategies must shift. I sense that it is time for the church to spiritually shift gears to avoid breaking down on the side of the road. We must get ready for the momentum of the next move of God.

This happens when "we all come into the unity of the faith and of the knowledge of the Son of God, into a complete man, to the measure of the stature of the fullness of Christ, so we may no longer be children, tossed here and there by waves and carried about with every wind of doctrine…[but] may grow up in all things into Him, who is the head, Christ Himself" (Eph. 4:13–15, MEV).

There must be a consistent, unified spiritual movement. As a former member of the US Army, I understand combat maneuvers. When a troop moves out, the synchronization of that movement is ignited through commands. These commands must be made by the designated leader, they must be given sharply, and they must be heard. The people of God cannot continue to sit in the spiritual lull we've been in.

I can't drive a car with a stick shift in the natural, but I understand how to shift gears in the spirit. Let's identify the problem at hand. While we have been sitting (full of power) at the stop signs and yield signs of this age, enemies of the gospel have created huge platforms with deafening demonic voices. These platforms have forced the church to succumb to being the silent majority in the grip of a loud minority. Let me be clear: there are more for us than there can ever be against us, yet we have been silenced! Why? Because of the spiritual lull!

But I am honored to announce that a new era has dawned. We are now in a season of fresh, twenty-twenty vision. There is a demand in the spirit realm for us to open our mouths and not just speak but pray out loud! This must be done through disciplines that include becoming good stewards of our words. We can no longer sit around like idling cars. We can no longer tolerate that which is designed by the flesh, the world, and the devil himself to slow us down and ultimately shut us down.

Speaking idle words of insincere, empty, religious rhetoric or powerless exaggeration does not frame the things of the kingdom. These kinds of words only distract and frame designs of failure. I declare that in the years to come the screeching sound of idle words that cause demonic idling will be no more.

It's dangerous to try to move to another level without understanding how to shift. The church at large must shift spiritually. To shift is to move from one place to another with special focus on a small distance.[1] Before a car reaches its maximum attainable speed, it must first shift gears, or it will break down. If the transition is not properly made, the gears can be jeopardized. This is called stripping the gears.

How many have stripped the spiritual gears in their ministries or even their lives because they did not understand the process of transition? Shifting is part of the process. Transition is the process or period of changing from one place, condition, or state to another.[2] It is definitely in order for me to talk about the

20

transition of God's people in the wilderness, which brings up the second thing that takes weight off your words in the spirit: murmuring and complaining.

MURMURING AND COMPLAINING

A murmurer is a person who habitually complains or grumbles. This person is a faultfinder, a grouch, and a whiner. I have ministered deliverance around the world for the past thirty years, and I can safely say it's easier to be delivered from perversion than from murmuring.

A murmurer is a cranky grouser who, like a crab, pulls others and even himself or herself down with words. The root of murmuring is in the mind. Either through imagery or magnification, the person creates scenarios that come from the heart, through the mind, and out of the mouth. These things escalate through demonic thoughts (thoughts that originate from the devil), mental locutions (a barrier created in the mind as a set way of doing things), and dark ideations (the forming of mental concepts and creation of images from the dark/negative side).

In the wilderness, the children of Israel brought curses upon themselves by complaining.

> When they came to Marah, they could not drink of the
> waters of Marah, for they were bitter. Therefore, the name of
> it was called Marah. So the people murmured against Moses,
> saying, "What shall we drink?"
>
> —EXODUS 15:23–24, MEV

21

In Exodus 16 and 17 the people complained that they would have preferred to stay in bondage in Egypt over going through the transition called the wilderness with Moses.

> And they took their journey from Elim, and all the congregation of the children of Israel came unto the wilderness of Sin, which is between Elim and Sinai, on the fifteenth day of the second month after their departing out of the land of Egypt. And the whole congregation of the children of Israel murmured against Moses and Aaron in the wilderness: And the children of Israel said unto them, Would to God we had died by the hand of the Lord in the land of Egypt, when we sat by the flesh pots, and when we did eat bread to the full; for ye have brought us forth into this wilderness, to kill this whole assembly with hunger.
>
> —EXODUS 16:1–3, KJV

In Numbers 14, even after the spies returned with news that the Promised Land actually existed and was as wonderful as they had been told, the people murmured against Moses and Aaron and slandered the land God had promised.

These passages of Scripture describe how the people responded to the pains of transition in the wilderness. Psalm 106:24–27 says they "despised the pleasant land" and "did not believe His word." The murmuring started in their tents (homes) because they did not hearken to the voice of the Lord. We must teach our families, especially our children, to be thankful and to fear God. Because the children of Israel did not reverence God and fear Him, the terror of the Lord came upon them. They had the audacity to believe God brought them all the way to the wilderness to let them die. If God wanted them to die, He could have left them in Egypt.

This is a word to the murmurer, the doubter, and the complainer in the church. God has brought you too far out of your mess to allow you to get stuck in the middle of what you're going through and never enter into His promise to you.

The Israelites even accused God of hating them and turning them over to the Amorites in the wilderness (Deut. 1:26–27). God is *agape*, and He loves His people unconditionally. Despite this, the Bible teaches that the Lord was angry with His people for these rebellious acts and lifted up His hand to overthrow them in the wilderness, to overthrow their seed among the nations, and to scatter them in the lands.

As usual, God's grace and mercy were sufficient, and He did not wipe out all their generations, but somebody had to pay. It's important to read this passage in *The Message* to understand how serious this was to God.

After the people of Israel grumbled and complained against God in the wilderness, Moses and Aaron fell on their faces in repentance, begging God to have mercy. He said, "I forgive them, honoring your words" (Num. 14:20). But then God told Moses and Aaron:

> How long is this going to go on, all this grumbling against me by this evil-infested community? I've had my fill of complaints from these grumbling Israelites. Tell them, As I live—GOD's decree—here's what I'm going to do: Your corpses are going to litter the wilderness—every one of you twenty years and older who was counted in the census, this whole generation of grumblers and grousers. Not one of you will enter the land and make your home there, the firmly and solemnly promised land, except for Caleb son of Jephunneh and Joshua son of Nun.
>
> Your children, the very ones that you said would be taken

23

for plunder, I'll bring in to enjoy the land you rejected while your corpses will be rotting in the wilderness. These children of yours will live as shepherds in the wilderness for forty years, living with the fallout of your whoring unfaithfulness until the last of your generation lies a corpse in the wilderness. You scouted out the land for forty days; your punishment will be a year for each day, a forty-year sentence to serve for your sins—a long schooling in my displeasure. I, GOD, have spoken.
—NUMBERS 14:26–35, MSG

The blessings of the Lord are yes and amen, but God is a jealous God, and He will have no other gods before Him, especially the gods of murmuring and complaining. This kind of rebellion caused God to allow everyone over twenty years old to die in the wilderness. An entire generation was destroyed.

Murmuring is dangerous and should be avoided at all costs. Below I have listed five manifestations of the murmuring spirit that we all must guard against.

Negative confessions that produce self-inflicted curses

Negative confessions such as "I can't do anything right" or "Nothing I do matters" cause arrows of destruction to shoot from the mouth and boomerang into the heart of the person who released the confession. A self-inflicted curse is a type of spiritual suicide because the person speaking the confession releases death against his or her own life. This stronghold of self-damnation can be difficult to be released from. The strength of this stronghold is that the person in bondage usually seeks help from the outside, but the solution to the problem is only inside. Self-inflicted curses through negative confession easily lodge inside the flesh of their victim and hide so well the person cannot recognize he or she is creating his or her own problems. This is demonic, and demons operate in the realm of the flesh. There is life and death in the power of the tongue. The greatest means of deliverance is for the murmurer to use the same tongue that created the bondage to loose deliverance.

Friendly fire

This term is usually used in military combat. It has sometimes been observed through the autopsies of casualties of war that soldiers were shot with the weapons of their colleagues. In other words, American soldiers were shot with American bullets. This is called friendly fire, and it happens in spiritual warfare also. It hurts when we take a hit in spiritual warfare, but it hurts worse when the arrow comes from someone we trusted. Friendly fire is high on the list of the enemy's favorite attacks. The devil hates real covenant, and he would do anything to destroy a vision from the inside. He wants the victims of friendly fire to think they can never trust anyone. He wants them to put up barriers to ward off even allies. Deliverance from friendly fire starts with being delivered from strange voices (voices other than God's; see John 10:1–5). When an anointed person of God avoids sitting at the yield sign of a strange voice, even when the arrows of friendly fire form, the person will not prosper.

Gossip

If a person commits a crime and another person assisted in the commission of that crime, that person is considered an accessory. This is similar to what happens when people participate in gossiping. Gossip is "casual or unconstrained conversation or reports about other people, typically involving details that are not confirmed as being true."[3] When we take part in these kinds of conversations, it can be deemed a curse because our words are not blessing anyone. Life is rooted in truth, and death is rooted in lies. Operating in lies leads to curses. Thus, a gossiper is an accessory to word curses.

God is calling His people to spread the gospel of Jesus Christ and not the gossip of the devil. If it is not the good news, it is bad news. Participating or even connecting with a gossiper incriminates.

Friend of the slanderer and demonic prognostication

We are living in the age of social media. People can literally log in and experience a virtual reality of what is happening on the streets, in our government forums, and even in our personal lives. The scary thing is that with the media frenzies we experience, people believe everything presented to them. I've been on the front lines of major events in Florida as a state representative. I'm sad to say that I have family members who are more likely to believe what is broadcast over the television or streamed over the internet than what I tell them—even if I was there. This is not because of my relationship with them. I'm referring to people I have good relationships with. They are mesmerized by social media. People become friends of the slanderer when they trust everything they see on social media and align with those speaking negativity instead of faith.

People have turned from reading their Bibles and spending time with God to spending time with Facebook, Twitter, and other social media platforms. Please don't misunderstand me. I see that these can be great platforms to win souls, but I'm afraid we may be losing more souls than we are winning. I know that spiritually speaking we always have more *for* us than *against* us. There is a battle raging, and the good news is that we win in the end. We have great things going on in different parts of the body of Christ, but we must connect and organize. One of us can put a thousand things to flight, and two can put ten thousand things to flight (Deut. 32:30). As I said previously, we must unite and promote the unity of faith. Believers will always have differences. Common denominators must be identified to solve our problems.

Exousia (secret intelligence) curses

Ephesians 6:12–18 talks about how we do not wrestle against flesh and blood. It goes on to say that the real battle is against principalities, powers, rulers of the darkness of this world, and spiritual wickedness in high places. In this passage of Scripture the word translated "powers" is *exousia*. A word study revealed that this term refers to something permissible or allowed; authority; liberty; denying the presence of opposition; ability, power, or strength; intensified power as it relates to authority in jurisdiction (a specialist such as a CIA or FBI agent in the natural); persons in authority; or powerful ones.[4] An *exousia* curse is a kind of familiar spirit.

Jesus said in Luke 10:19, "Behold, I give unto you power to tread on serpents and scorpions, and over all the power of the enemy: and nothing shall by any means hurt you" (KJV). This means that whatever comes against us is already defeated if it challenges the authority given to us as believers. Power is mentioned twice in this verse, but the two Greek words used are not the same. The first power is *exousia*, and the second is *dunamis*, which relates to miracle-working power.[5] This word stresses ability but not necessarily accomplishment. *Strong's Exhaustive Concordance* refers to *dunamis* as intrinsic power, which means it belongs to the nature of a thing or should come naturally, as an endowment.

Putting it in layman's terms, it should be the norm for a believer to walk in miracles. *Dunamis* means having the spirit of strength, being fearless when opposed, and void of cowardice. *Dunamis* comes with a supernatural boldness for those who would dare to tap into it. It releases an anointing that takes a normal individual above and beyond what a natural man or woman is capable of doing. *Dunamis* is seen throughout the New Testament when the apostles and prophets were empowered by the Holy Spirit. They walked in the almighty energy of the Messiah that produced wonder-working deeds and unquestionable miracles.

Considering all of this, Luke 10:19 says Jesus gave the believer *exousia* (a position of authority that includes *dunamis*) to tread on serpents and authority over the *dunamis* (counterfeit miracle-working power) of the enemy. It is no secret that the devil has power, but in the name of Jesus and through the blood of Jesus, we have authority over all the power of the devil.

Watch as well as pray! Not everyone who prays in tongues is of God. Not everyone who falls out under the power is getting up with the Holy Ghost. The sorcerers of Egypt threw down their rods, and they turned into snakes. Moses threw down his one rod, and it became a snake that swallowed the counterfeits. Charismatic witchcraft is a reality.

There are people who were called by God but answered the call of the devil. Please don't be confused, and I definitely don't want you to be afraid. The counterfeit does exist, but if you walk in your authority as a believer, you will rule over the power of the enemy. There is a demonic *exousia* and a Holy Ghost *exousia*. There is a demonic *dunamis* and a Holy Ghost *dunamis*. For everything God created, the devil has a counterfeit. Watch my words closely: God creates because He is the Creator, and the devil counterfeits because he is a liar and a copycat.

An *exousia* (secret intelligence) curse operates in people who use their anointing on the dark side. The gifts and callings of God are without repentance (Rom. 11:29). The Greek word translated "gifts" in that verse is *charisma*, and it refers to "grace or gifts denoting extraordinary powers, distinguishing certain Christians and enabling them to serve the church of Christ, the reception of which is due to the power of divine grace operating on their souls by the Holy Spirit."[6] God gives gifts, and He does not repent or take them back. Gifted people can leave God and continue to operate under a dark covering. I relate the word *exousia* to an authoritative specialist such as an FBI or CIA agent. These agents operate in power but mostly behind the scenes.

Be careful of people in your life who operate in legitimate authority originating from God with illegitimate covering from the dark side. People slip to the other side knowingly and unknowingly all the time. They manifest as covenant breakers, backbiters, backstabbers, Judas spirits, two-timers, snitches, talebearers, liars, frauds, deceivers, deserters, infidels, sellouts, double-crossers, business crooks, people of great guile, and demonically planted informers. Regardless of the manifestation, they are on assignment to destroy lives, so beware.

There is a connection between roots and fruits. Our words bring forth the fruit of either life or death. When our words breed life, that good fruit continues to grow. On the other hand, when our words breed death, a desolation or barrenness occurs that creates a desert place. By the words of almighty God creation was framed. God placed that same creative force in our tongues. Pray out loud with a disciplined tongue so you can live in the fullness of God's promises.

LET'S PRAY OUT LOUD!

Father God, in the precious name of Jesus, thank You for anointing me to walk circumspectly, as the days are evil. I praise You for breaking every limitation off my life and giving me the tongue of the learned. Thank You for undergirding me in agape love. I renounce every noisome sound, clanging cymbal, and annoying distraction. Father, create a God-ordained platform rooted in the breadth, length, depth, and height of Your love. Your love covers a multitude of sins, and I prophesy that my generations will love You and sin not. I declare that goodness and mercy shall follow me and my seed all the days of our lives. We will not be murmurers in the tents. No idle words or idolatrous thoughts will plague us.

I commit to moving with what the Spirit of God is doing in the kingdom. Every demonic stop sign or any sign (in the spirit) that causes me to falsely yield or hinder my progression is bound and blocked in Jesus' name. I have victory over every antichrist spirit, anti-progression spirit, and all enemies of the gospel. I use the power of my tongue to bless the pleasant land that You promised me. I will hearken to Your voice and believe the Word of the Lord. I will not be overthrown in the wilderness. My seed will not be overthrown among the nations, and my family will not be scattered in the lands. In Jesus' name, amen.

DECLARATIONS FOR GUARDING AND
DISCIPLINING YOUR TONGUE

Make the following declarations out loud as often as you need to. If you confess the Word of God consistently, it will cause you to guard your heart and tongue so you will not sin against God with murmuring and complaining.

- The Lord shall fight for me, and I shall hold my peace (Exod. 14:14).

- Lord, "teach me, and I will hold my tongue; cause me to understand wherein I have erred" (Job 6:24).

- I stand in awe and sin not; I commune with my own heart upon my bed and am still (Ps. 4:4).

- For they speak not peace: but they devise deceitful matters against them that are quiet in the land. Father, I choose to speak peace (Ps. 35:20).

- I will rest in the Lord and wait patiently for Him; I will not fret because of him who prospers in his way or because of the man who brings wicked devices to pass. I will trust in the Lord (Ps. 37:7).

- I will be still and know that You are God. You will be exalted among the nations; You will be exalted on the earth (Ps. 46:10).

- "The wise in heart will receive commands, but a prating fool will fall." I choose to be wise in heart and will receive Your commandments (Prov. 10:8).

- I will not be void of wisdom and despise my neighbor; I hold my peace because I am a person of understanding (Prov. 11:12).

- "He that keepeth his mouth keepeth his life: but he that openeth wide his lips shall have destruction." I keep my mouth and therefore keep my life. I am not one who opens her lips wide and reaps destruction (Prov. 13:3, KJV).

- Your Word says "a fool uttereth all his mind: but a wise man keepeth it in till afterwards." I am wise, and I keep my thoughts till afterward (Prov. 29:11).

- You will keep me in perfect peace because my mind is stayed on You and because I trust in You (Isa. 26:3).

- I hope and quietly wait for the salvation of the Lord (Lam. 3:26).

- I will let no corrupt communication proceed out of my mouth but that which is good for the use of edifying, that it may minister grace unto the hearers (Eph. 4:29).

- I study to be quiet and to do my own business and to work with my own hands, as the Lord commanded (1 Thess. 4:11–12).

- I will be "swift to hear, slow to speak, slow to wrath" (Jas. 1:19).

CHAPTER 3

PRAY OUT LOUD AS
A TRUE BELIEVER

I HAVE NEVER BEEN one to focus on the end of the world, but I can attest that we are living in what are called the last days. Now more than ever Christians need their voices to be heard. But in order to have a legitimate platform to pray out loud, a person must be a true believer.

Ephesians 2:8–9 says, "For by grace you have been saved through faith, and this is not of yourselves. It is the gift of God, not of works, so that no one should boast" (MEV). The Bible makes it clear that our good works don't save us, and 2 Corinthians 3:5 tells us that we are not "sufficient in ourselves to take credit for anything of ourselves, but our sufficiency is from God" (MEV). This means we cannot boast in our own goodness.

The world is changing around us, and the church is facing challenges we've never encountered before, but what it means to be a true believer has not changed. True believers still have certain characteristics.

TRUE BELIEVERS WILL FACE OPPOSITION

Matthew 10:22 says true believers will be hated for Jesus' name-sake, but only the one who endures to the end will be saved. I always say we are not saved; we are being saved. Salvation is a continual process of endurance, and true believers never stop reaching toward the mark. Paul made it clear that he could not sit back and be comfortable in his place in God. He had to press toward the mark for the prize of the high calling of God in Christ Jesus (Phil. 3:14). The word *press* means to "move or cause to move into a position of contact with something by exerting continuous physical force."[1] Often this force must be exerted because of opposition.

One of the main signs of true, born-again believers is that they will have opposition. The reason Paul had to press was that there were obstacles and hindrances between him and the mark. These obstacles and barriers are called distractions, and they are demonically set in place to stop us from reaching the mark. Because there's opposition ahead of us as believers, it is very important that we not walk alongside the opposition.

Second Corinthians 6:14 warns us not to be unequally yoked with unbelievers. The Word of the Lord goes on to say, "What fellowship has righteousness with lawlessness? And what communion has light with darkness?" (MEV). A yoke is a wooden bar that joins two oxen to each other. It's a connector that can overpower or pull a person in a particular direction. As believers, with all the opposition ahead of us, it will be dangerous to walk side by side with people who can pull us in the wrong direction. I pray this message is getting your attention. Be careful not to connect or yoke with any person, place, or thing that will pull you toward the wrong course. Of course that begs the question "If you need to avoid relationships in which you are unequally yoked, how can you tell which people, places, and things to be yoked to?"

TRUE BELIEVERS HAVE SIGNS FOLLOWING THEM

Mark 16:17–18 says, "And these signs shall follow them that believe; in my name they shall cast out devils; they shall speak with new tongues: they shall take up serpents, and if they drink any deadly thing, it shall not hurt them. They shall lay hands on the sick and they shall recover" (KJV). This passage of Scripture tells us who believers are. Believers do not run after signs as the Bible says evil men do; instead, signs follow them! Based on the passage from Mark 16,

- believers cast out devils,
- believers speak with new tongues,
- believers take up serpents,
- believers can drink any deadly thing, and it shall not hurt them, and
- believers lay hands on the sick, and they recover.

I've been saved for over thirty years, and one of the most baffling things to me is that people who call themselves believers don't believe Mark 16:17–18!

TRUE BELIEVERS FACE PERSECUTION

It's amazing that the world mocks anything believers are called to do. They come against anything that demonstrates the power of God, but they justify and support anything that has a form of godliness and denies God's power. I think I am safe in saying I'm a rare person in that I am a pastor who also serves in the political arena. For four years, I was a member of the Florida

House of Representatives. I am a Black female Democrat, and I pray in tongues and cast out devils. As far as I know, I am the first, and I know I'm correct in saying this has not been popular with most of my Democratic colleagues.

They celebrate the first gay men and women in the Legislature but have no tolerance for a demon buster. True believers will face persecution. Consider the following verses.

- "Blessed are they which are persecuted for righteousness' sake: for theirs is the kingdom of heaven" (Matt. 5:10, KJV).

- "Blessed are ye, when men shall hate you, and when they shall separate you from their company, and shall reproach you, and cast out your name as evil, for the son of man's sake" (Luke 6:22, KJV).

- "If the world hates you, you know that it hated me before it hated you" (John 15:18).

- "Yea, and all that will live godly in Christ Jesus shall suffer persecution" (2 Tim 3:12, KJV).

At the end of this chapter I include several scriptures for you to confess out loud, especially during times of persecution. Whenever you do, also take a minute to praise God because if you are being persecuted for your faith, God is about to bless your boots off. But this blessing is conditional on you blessing those who attempt to destroy you. (See Romans 12:14.) As crazy as it may sound, you must begin to take pleasure in the arrows that are shot against your life. I prophesy over your head that no weapons formed against you will prosper, and because you've been reviled for Christ's sake, you will receive "mega-more" and manifold blessings. Your latter will be greater than your former, and eyes have not seen nor ears heard what God is about to do for you.

It is no secret that believers will be drawn together by the persecution they endure from those who hate Christ. The good news is that favor accompanies persecution. Walk out your persecution and walk in favor. Whether you are being persecuted by family members, your job, your community, or even everyday life itself, press toward the mark.

I'm qualified to talk about being persecuted as a believer. During my tenure as an elected official, numerous false allegations were made against me. I had to learn to endure the defamation and accusations my enemies leveled against me back-to-back. I have never been through an election without my opponents involving me in a manufactured scandal. But as I write this book, I am an overcomer and more than a conqueror as I continue to press toward the mark.

The name of the strongman that continually sets its ugly face against me is religious persecution. Political entities, special interests, and those with antichrist agendas have hijacked the mainstream media to work against true believers or anyone who supports or associates with them.

By God's grace and favor, I was able to operate as an elected official for nearly a decade. That favor allowed me to write legislation to put prayer back in school in Florida, have "In God We Trust" conspicuously displayed in all public schools, be the prime sponsor of a huge criminal justice reform bill, get $2,125,000 for a man wrongfully incarcerated for forty-three years, and allocate millions of dollars to programs run by everyday people for community outreach in my city. Much more was accomplished, but these are the highlights of my four years as a state representative. They are the fruits of my labor, and they came with a lot of hard times, hatred, and opposition.

I'm sad to say that if you really love Jesus and are a true believer, you must learn to be hated, but be encouraged. As I mentioned previously, Luke 10:19 says, "Behold I give unto you power to tread on serpents and scorpions, and over all the power of the enemy: and nothing shall by no means hurt you" (KJV). And Romans 16:20 says, "And the God of peace will crush Satan under your feet shortly." Hang in there. Your breakthrough is about to come.

TRUE BELIEVERS ARE KNOWN BY THEIR FRUIT

In addition to being known by the persecution we face, true believers will know one another by the fruit they bear. Matthew 7:16–20 (MEV) explains this clearly.

> Do men gather grapes from thorns, or figs from thistles? Even so, every good tree bears good fruit. But a corrupt tree bears evil fruit. A good tree cannot bear evil fruit, nor can a corrupt tree bear good fruit. Every tree that does not bear good fruit is cut down and thrown into the fire. Therefore, by their fruit you will know them.

Galatians chapter 5 highlights the fruit of the born-again believer as love, joy, peace, longsuffering, kindness, goodness, faithfulness, gentleness, and self-control (vv. 22–23). I would also like to add that there is a kingdom language whereby believers know one another. We can touch and agree because we speak the same tongue and travel on the same circuit. We can walk together in agreement because we are receiving the glory from the same spout. No longer do we walk according to the course of this world and the prince of the power of the air who rules over the careless, rebellious, and unbelieving. We are the children of God, who care, obey, and believe.

TRUE BELIEVERS ARE ON ASSIGNMENT

Another way to know true believers is to look for those on assignment. Matthew 28:19–20 says it best: "Go ye therefore, and teach all nations, baptizing them in the name of the Father and of the Son and of the Holy Ghost: Teaching them to observe all things whatsoever I have commanded you: and, lo, I am with you always, even unto the end of the world" (KJV). These words are to strengthen you in your calling. God is saying that wherever we go, we must take the gospel of Jesus Christ with us.

There is another gospel being preached in the land, one with a different Holy Ghost and a false Christ. There are spirits of seduction in the land, so we must obey the high calling and go forth, speaking truth and walking in discernment. Beware of those who act like believers, look like believers, and even try to speak the language of the kingdom. First John 4:1 warns us not to believe every spirit but to "try the spirits whether they are of God: because many false prophets are gone out into the world" (KJV). I like the way *The Message* puts it: "My dear friends, don't believe everything you hear. Carefully weigh and examine what people tell you. Not everyone who talks about God comes from God. There are a lot of lying preachers loose in the world."

Second Timothy 3:5 speaks of those who have a form of godliness but deny the power of God. Timothy teaches that they are not believers, and we must turn away from them. Christianity has split into so many factions that it could be confusing to an everyday person. Acts 11:26 tells us the term Christian was coined at Antioch. Christian persecution became so bad that believers had to hide out and use certain symbols to identify one another.

Eventually it was not important whether people called themselves Christians; the question asked to ensure a person was a true believer was, "Do you know the way?" Jesus said, "I am the way, the truth, and the life. No one comes to the Father except through Me" (John 14:6, MEV). As you come to the end of this chapter, I ask the same question of you: Are you a Christian in name only, or do you know the way?

PRAYER TO AFFIRM YOUR IDENTITY AS A TRUE BELIEVER

Father, in the name of Jesus, I renounce nominal Christianity. I speak the language of the kingdom and no longer walk according to the course of this world under the rulership of the prince of the power of the air. I renounce carelessness, rebellion, and unbelief. I am a good tree, and I cannot bear evil fruit. Love, joy, peace, longsuffering, kindness, goodness, faithfulness, gentleness, and self-control are my portion. I touch and agree and form a circle with my fellow believers, and together we have power over all the power of the enemy, and the God of peace will crush Satan under our feet shortly. In Jesus' name I pray, amen.

CONFESSIONS FOR BUILDING FAITH
IN THE MIDST OF PERSECUTION

- I am blessed because I'm being persecuted for righteousness' sake; mine is the kingdom of heaven (Matt 5:10).

- "I take pleasure in infirmities, in reproaches, in necessities, in persecutions, in distresses for Christ's sake; for when I am weak, then am I strong" (2 Cor. 12:10).

- I know that all who will live godly in Christ Jesus shall suffer persecution. I choose to live godly; therefore, I suffer persecution (2 Tim 3:12).

- Though the world hates me, I know it hated You before it hated me (John 15:18).

- I am blessed when people hate me and when they separate me from their company, reproach me, and cast out my name as evil for the Son of Man's sake (Luke 6:22).

- Nothing shall separate me from the love of Christ, not tribulation or distress or persecution or famine or nakedness or peril or sword. No, in all these things I am more than a conqueror through Him who loves me. "For I am persuaded that neither death nor life, neither angels nor principalities nor powers, neither things present nor things to come, neither height nor depth, nor any other created thing, shall be able to separate me from the love of God, which is in Christ Jesus my Lord" (Rom. 8:35–39, MEV).

- I am blessed when people revile me and persecute me and say all manner of evil against me falsely for the Lord's sake (Matt. 5:11).

- "No one who has left house or brothers or sisters or father or mother or wife or children or lands, for [Christ's] sake and the gospel's, who shall not receive a hundredfold now in this time—houses and brothers and sisters and mothers and children and lands, with persecutions—and in the age to come, eternal life" (Mark 10:29–30).

- I will bless those who persecute me; I will bless and curse not (Rom. 12:14).

- "My times are in Your hand; deliver me from the hand of my enemies, and from those who persecute me" (Ps. 31:15).

- I will be sober and vigilant "because [my] adversary the devil walks about like a roaring lion, seeking whom he may devour" (1 Pet. 5:8).

CHAPTER 4

PRAY OUT LOUD IN THE SPIRIT

SOME WASTE COMES from overuse. Water, for instance, can be wasted when we let the faucet just run. But waste can also come from a lack of use or negligence. For example, many people waste time by simply being idle. But of all the things that go to waste, I believe the greatest in all of creation is when Spirit-filled believers do not use the power of their prayer language.

Praying in tongues, or praying in the Spirit, has impacted my spiritual life more than anything I have experienced. It is also one of the most powerful tools for overcoming subliminal fears and spiritual skeletons that plague one's life.

Praying in tongues has several benefits.

- When we pray in tongues, we speak mysteries unto God, and we speak directly to Him (1 Cor. 14:2).

- When we pray in tongues, we ignite the atmosphere for whatever God is doing (Acts 2).

- When we pray in tongues, we build up our most holy faith and edify and strengthen ourselves (1 Cor. 14:4; Jude 20).

- When we pray in tongues, we tame the unruliness of the tongue, as James taught (Jas. 3:1–3).

- When we pray in tongues, we dress ourselves with spiritual armor of God (Eph. 6:18).

- When we pray in tongues, we can pray without ceasing (1 Thess. 5:17).

- When we pray in tongues, we have access to the ability to interpret what God is saying (1 Cor. 12, 14).

- Praying in tongues or in the Spirit also brings us into unity with God when we pray privately and into unity with one another when we pray corporately.

I believe being filled with the Holy Spirit is a mandate for believers. Some would beg to differ with me, but I believe I can present a pretty good case. I'm not saying a person who does not speak in tongues is not saved. I'm also not saying that just because people speak in tongues, they are better off. I am saying that a person who neglects to receive the infilling of the Holy Ghost and this part of the covering of God's armor will not experience God's best for their spiritual well-being.

My prayer is that if you are not currently filled with the Holy Spirit with the evidence of speaking in tongues, you will be praying in tongues by the end of this chapter. I also pray that whether it is your first filling or a fresh infilling, you will experience the joy of having rivers of living waters flow out of your inner man. Jesus said, "He who believes in Me, as the Scripture has said, out of his heart shall flow rivers of living water" (John 7:38, MEV). The King James Version says, "Out of his belly shall flow rivers of living water."

My favorite saying is that still waters run deep. Those who receive Jesus into their lives do have water in their bellies, but they cannot operate in the fullness of the deliverance God has for them until those waters start flowing. I decree and declare the flow of God's Spirit is running out of your belly! There is a difference between a river and a ditch. Both can contain water, but in a river there is a flow. This flow pushes out the trash. This is what I mean by saying still waters run deep. Without the flow, the trash just sits there and turns into pollution.

Not only do we need to be filled with the Holy Spirit, but we also must have a continual flow or a fresh infilling to refresh our souls. Rivers of living water push out spirits of depression and suicide. This refreshing experience becomes a lifestyle that is contagious; if used properly, it will affect the people you come in contact with. I have many testimonies of God moving miraculously when I prayed in tongues.

THE POWER OF PRAYING IN THE SPIRIT

One of the first instances was when I was newly saved and stationed in Frankfurt, Germany. As a matter of fact, it was the day I was going to preach my first sermon to start Spoken Word Ministries. Mike was my only child at the time, and he was living with me in the city. (We called it the economy.) In other words, we were not living on the military installation but in local housing.

I was fasting and had been praying in tongues nonstop all day long. I was so excited about my first ministry assignment. Mike was at the apartment because a neighbor in our building was watching out for him. (It was a very safe environment.)

Before I left, I fried some french fries for Mike, and without realizing it, I left the pot of grease on the stove. I drove a couple of hours away and ministered at a prison and returned home hours later to a smoky apartment. I was told that the pot sat smoldering on the stove for hours as Mike slept in the back room. Smoke began to fill the apartment building, and eventually my neighbor smelled it. Because the door to my apartment was unlocked, my neighbor's husband was able to crawl on the floor through the apartment to rescue Mike. They were also able to turn off the stove.

The miracle was that not only was Mike unharmed, but the pot never burned! I still have that pot today. It is a white pot with flowers on it, and it reminds me of how God's miracle-working power will defy all odds. Mike had no problems with smoke inhalation, and the kitchen never caught on fire—and the pot sat on the hot stove for hours!

I know some people may have a hard time believing what I'm saying, but those who know God know He can do anything! When my home was in danger, I did not cease praying in tongues. I didn't know what was happening with my natural mind, but I believe my spirit was connecting with the Holy Spirit and saying, "God, put Your angels around that hot grease burning on the stove. Don't allow that pot to catch on fire. Keep Mike, and let no harm come nigh my dwelling!"

The German family that was watching Mike knew what time I left and that the pot never caught on fire. I was a witness for Christ to their souls. You know I gave God all the honor, glory, and praise!

I want to share two other miracles I experienced while praying in tongues. One had to do with one of my sisters who didn't know the Lord at the time. I know that God's hand is heavy on my sister's life because the devil was always trying to snuff her out. Her story is a reminder that we must be sensitive to the intercessory aspect of praying in tongues, which Paul described in Romans 8:26–27:

> Likewise the Spirit also helps in our weaknesses. For we do not know what we should pray for as we ought, but the Spirit Himself makes intercession for us with groanings which cannot be uttered. Now He who searches the hearts knows what the mind of the Spirit is, because He makes intercession for the saints according to the will of God.

Truly the Holy Spirit made intercession for me as I prayed in tongues while moving into an apartment in Jacksonville with my sister after leaving the military and returning home. I was fresh off the plane, and my sister was on a trip to South Florida for what we called the police Olympics.

As I was unpacking and settling into the apartment, I could not stop praying in tongues. Let me stop right here to offer some advice. If you ever feel the unction to pray in the Spirit, *pray*— and pray out loud! If you are not in a place to do it, get where you can. It can be a matter of life and death. I had been praying in tongues for hours. The people helping me move in were looking at me side-eyed, but I kept praying. Then I received a phone call that removed the question marks from over everyone's head. My sister called with a creepy sound in her voice. She was staying in a hotel with several other officers, and a band of robbers had infiltrated the hotel rooms where the officers were fellowshipping, invaded room by room, and tied the officers up.

They robbed them, and my sister heard them speak of killing everyone to leave no witnesses.

As they were tying my sister's hands behind her back, one of the robbers said, "Man, she so fine; don't tie her up too tight." They left her bands loose and exited the room. Despite the trauma my sister was experiencing, she was able to get loose and use a cigarette lighter to set off the sprinklers in the room. The robbers fled, and not one person was physically injured. Thank You, Holy Spirit! That day I knew why I was focused on praying in the Spirit. I was not talking to anyone. I just continued to pray until God gave me the release to stop. I call this "praying through."

Often we have prayer times and prayer watches, and we "hit it and quit it." We are not living in times for "hit it and quit it" prayers or "boom bam, thank you, ma'am" intercession. We must pray through! To pray through a thing means to pray until the assignment is completed or until the Holy Spirit gives us a release. This is called praying without understanding. It is the most powerful weapon God has given believers.

As I mentioned previously, Mark 16:17 says, "And these signs shall follow them that believe; in my name they shall cast out devils; they shall speak with *new tongues*" (KJV, emphasis added). Whether we are speaking in new tongues, other tongues, foreign tongues, tongues of fire, angelic tongues, or divers kinds of tongues, as long as we're doing it as the Spirit gives utterance, it is a blessing.

Acts 2:4 declares that the people of the New Testament church were filled with the Holy Spirit and began to speak with other tongues as the Spirit gave them utterance. Acts 19:2 asks, "Have you received the Holy Spirit since you believed?" This means people can believe and not be filled with the Holy Spirit. I choose not just to believe but to be a *believer*! There is a difference.

I'm an ordained minister of the gospel of Jesus Christ. I'm a preacher! To fulfill the mandate I have been given, I must do what I am called to do. Being ordained doesn't make me a preacher. I'm a preacher because I preach! Action accompanies the title. Can you imagine a preacher in name only, someone who doesn't preach or minister? This is how I can't imagine believers who don't do what God set them in the earth realm to do. We are not called to just believe; we are called to be believers! Praying in tongues had a whole lot to do with being a believer in the New Testament church, and it should have a lot to do with being a believer who makes his or her voice heard in the world we live in today.

LET'S PRAY OUT LOUD!

Father God, in the name of Jesus, I thank You for filling me with the Holy Spirit with the evidence of speaking in other tongues (or I thank You for a fresh infilling of the Holy Ghost). Lord, I thank You for the gifts of the Spirit that are flowing fluidly through me. Out of my belly shall flow rivers of living water. These rivers are pushing that trash out of my life and bringing forth a refreshing flow of the Holy Ghost.

I renounce every dark shadow, skeleton, secret, closet bondage, and subliminal fear that would attempt to lie dormant in my life. I declare that every hidden bondage or assignment that exists in or around my life will be made manifest, and every secret set in place to bring harm will be brought to light. I decree and declare that I submit to the Holy Spirit to help me in my weakness, and as I don't know what to pray, He will make intercession for me.

God, I thank You for top-secret security prayers with groanings that cannot be uttered with natural words. Holy Spirit, pray through my inner being to make intercession on behalf of the saints according to the will of God. I walk under the covering and in the anointing and authority of the believer to release my prayer language as the Spirit gives utterance. I release this anointing in my personal life to build up my most holy faith, as intercession to save and support those around me, and into the atmosphere to create an environment conducive to the spiritual climate God has ordained. This I pray in Jesus' name, amen.

CHAPTER 5

PRAY OUT LOUD IN THE MORNING

MOST OF MY life, I was not what you would call a morning person. But when I got saved, the Lord started waking me up in the wee hours of the morning, and over time—I don't even remember when it happened—I became a commander of the morning. It changed my life forever.

There is no way I could have attempted to write a book on prayer without including the discipline of commanding the morning. First let's take a look at a foundational scripture:

> Have you commanded the morning since your days began,
> and caused the dawn to know its place, that it might take hold
> of the ends of the earth, and the wicked be shaken out of it?
> —JOB 38:12–13

In Job 38 God was essentially checking Job. God was reminding Job that He was the Creator. What was going on between God and Job is not where I want to focus. I want to direct your attention to the question God asked Job: "Have you commanded the morning since your days began?"

After asking this question, God went on to explain that commanding the morning makes the dawn know its place that the light from the breaking of dawn/dayspring might take hold of the ends of the earth and shake the wicked (those who devise evil in the night) from the four corners of creation.

51

As God was lightly rebuking Job, He was also giving Job a powerful revelation about how to attack the high places and shift things in the spirit in the wee hours of the morning. I don't know how Job responded to this revelation, but when I read Job 38, I grabbed hold of this principle and never let it go. I am a commander of the morning, and I invite you to become one also.

We don't have to wait to see what hand our day deals out to us! We can become early risers and use the power of life and death that is in our tongues to establish our days and set atmospheres to create a new climate in our regions.

When God created mankind, He gave us dominion over the air, earth, and sea and even what is under the earth and sea. (See Genesis 1:26–28.) Let me be clear: God did not give this dominion to men, women, or even Christians; He gave dominion to mankind, and some use it demonically to control people's destinies. God wants us to take authority over the elements of the morning and release prayers that will bring *heaven down to earth*. Many are trying to get to heaven, but God is anointing us to bring heaven here!

God has not finished what He is doing through us in the earth realm. We don't have to just accept whatever the enemy throws upon us. We can unlock the will of God in the heavens and walk in His will right here on earth.

It's important to note that demonic checkpoints in the heavenlies have been used to manipulate the outcome of our days. No more! You can pray out loud and command your morning. Wicked men have tapped into the supernatural to attempt to control our destinies from the dark side. We are no longer ignorant of the enemy's devices, and we are charging the gates of the second heaven early in the morning.

Perhaps you already know the power of commanding the morning because you've been getting up at 5:00 a.m. and commanding the morning for over twenty years. You know it's a vehicle God can use to take your prayer life to another level, but now it's time to upgrade. In the natural if someone is still driving a vehicle from the year 1999, he or she may run into a few problems. If the vehicle has been maintained, it may suffice, but we are not reaching for good enough. We are pursuing deeper depths and higher heights.

God is doing a new thing! He is not changing the word He spoke in Job 38:12–13; He is changing us. He's causing us to get new revelation out of what He is doing in the morning in the earth realm. When we commanded the morning in 1999, it was great, but I fully expect God to do things today that He has never done before. I believe that eyes have not seen, nor ears heard, neither has it entered into the hearts of men the things that He has in store for us who love Him (1 Cor. 2:9).

I'm ready to pray into the earth realm whatever God wants to do, but I need intercessors from around the world to make covenant with me in commanding the morning. I'm praying for intercessors who will rise and shine in the light of the revelation of this powerful message. We are living in challenging times, but I am up for the challenge. I realize the message I'm releasing is not common or comfortable and is not taught in many churches, but through activation, impartation, and training, we can change that. I'm sure most would agree with me that we are not having church as usual these days and status quo ministry is a thing of the past.

53

THE FOURTH WATCH

The New Testament speaks of four watches, which are understood to be from 6:00 p.m. to 9:00 p.m., from 9:00 p.m. to midnight, from midnight to 3:00 a.m., and from 3:00 a.m. to 6:00 a.m. I said earlier that God wants our intercession to bring heaven down to earth. Jesus told us to pray that the kingdom would come so the will of God would be done on earth (Matt. 6:10). By hijacking the airways of the early-morning watch, we bring heaven down to earth. Yes, that's right—we're taking over the fourth watch of the day.

I don't believe it's by chance that Jesus walked on the water during the fourth watch, the watch of miracles. I liken the fourth prayer watch to the fourth quarter of a football game. It doesn't matter what has happened during the first three quarters; it's all about the fourth quarter. During the fourth quarter, teams that were losing can come from behind and win. In the sports arena this is called a new day. God is doing a new thing in the earth realm, and we need to loudly declare to the enemy and his devils that it is a new day. We win in the end.

Anything can happen in the fourth watch! There is no losing in God. No matter what the situation looks like at night, no matter how much weeping you endure, joy (a new day) comes in the morning (Ps. 30:5).

Micah 2:1 speaks of enemies who devise wicked schemes against the innocent at night. Psalm 91:5 speaks of the terror that comes by night. Between 6:00 p.m. and 8:30 p.m., the day starts moving toward darkness, and the wicked lurk. They have a saying in the world that the freaks come out at night. This is one of the reasons people cannot sleep at night—the tormentors are loosed. The creepy crawlers, the things that go bump in the night and hide in closets, manifest during the night season. Curses and sickness are seeded and even heighten during the dark time of the night. But when we command our morning, those prayers take hold of the four corners of creation and shake out the wickedness manufactured and fabricated at night.

EXERCISE DOMINION

Rising early in the morning to pray is all about dominion. God gave us dominion over *everything* He created. He put the power of dominion in our mouths. Jesus told the disciples they could have a level of authority to speak to mountains and those mountains would be removed (Matt 21:21). The morning provides a mountain-moving platform for intercession. The light shakes evil plans devised at night from the four corners of creation, and the dayspring moves every mountain of rebellion. We can use our mouths to speak things that are not as though they already exist (Rom. 4:17). There is life and death in the power of the tongue (Prov. 18:21).

Men operated in this kind of dominion throughout the Bible. Elijah commanded the heavens to close and not rain for three and a half years, and the heavens obeyed (Jas. 5:17). Joshua spoke to the sun and the moon and commanded them to stand still (Josh. 10:12). As believers, we have the same dominion today! Let's rise up early in the morning and *exercise* it. No matter what we are going through in America today, this nation is still a land of milk and honey. We live in a promised land, and God has given us authority to possess everything in it. A good way to start is by praying out loud in the morning!

Kingsley Fletcher is a powerful man of authority. He is a king in Ghana and an apostle and prophet stationed in America. He holds authority in the spirit and in the natural. I'm humbled that the Lord has blessed me to have both natural and spiritual authority too as a former commissioner and state representative and as an apostle of Jesus Christ.

Pastor Fletcher once gave me a spiritual nugget I will never forget. He said everything God created has ears. That is true. If it weren't, the things God created would not have heard Him when He spoke them into existence. At creation God spoke to things that were not when He said, "Let there be...," and creation heard Him and began to "be."

In the church El Shaddai is often understood to mean the all-sufficient One, or the God of more than enough. I was talking to a friend of mine who is a Hebrew scholar, and he said that interpretation is not exactly correct. He said Shaddai means that God said, "Enough!" He explained that if God had not said, "Enough," things would have continued to be created. When God speaks, all of creation is attentive.

God is great, and that greatness is inside of us. After twenty years of commanding the morning, I am recruiting you, the reader of this book, to become a commander of the morning. Join this mighty army of the Lord as we

- grab hold of the wings of the morning,
- speak to the ears of the morning, and
- impregnate the womb of the morning.

56

Open your mouth, early riser, and allow the spermatic words released in the heavenlies to speak on your behalf. In Psalm 19:1–3, David proclaimed that the heavens declare God's glory.

> The heavens declare the glory of God; and the firmament shows His handiwork. Day unto day utters speech, and night unto night reveals knowledge. There is no speech nor language where their voice is not heard.

If the skies have a voice and declare the goodness of God, just imagine how much God can do through us when we open our mouths. Pray out loud, saints! Psalm 119:147–148 says that we can "anticipate the dawning of the morning," and our eyes can prevent the night watches of evil watchmen. Pray before the sun sets, saints! When we get up in the wee hours of the morning, we blind the third eye of the enemy that heads up the night watches against our destinies.

In May 2006 tens of thousands of intercessors stood with me in prayer as I declared on worldwide television in the early-morning hours that the brutal hurricane seasons we were having would cease. I prophesied that in America we would not have a hurricane hit land and cause devastation for three years. I stood on James 5:7, which says Elijah was a man of like passions when he closed the heavens from rain on Mount Carmel.

After I declared that God would give our nation a break from devastating hurricanes, the meteorologists predicted that the hurricane season would be worse than ever. They predicted that eight to ten major storms would come out of the Atlantic and possibly hit land. That number eventually went down to between seven and nine.[1] But we commanded the morning every day, declaring that zero hurricanes would have a catastrophic impact on the nation, and zero it was for three years.[2]

Hurricane Katrina and several other storms had hit us back-to-back. Our lifestyles were interrupted by storm after storm. So a band of intercessors stood on the Word of God. We drove from coast to coast, stretching our hands toward the storms in the early-morning hours and agreeing with what was prophesied. We prayed against storms hitting the coast of the Carolinas, coming through South Florida, devastating the Gulf region, or affecting other parts of the country.

I was visiting Pastor John Hagee's church in San Antonio, Texas, in 2017 when the calls came for Houston to be evacuated in advance of Hurricane Harvey. Chuck Pierce, a prophetic minister who leads Glory of Zion International Ministries in the Dallas area, called and instructed me to go to a specific riverbank an hour away to throw salt in the river and prophesy over the waters. I drove to the designated point with some intercessors, and we obeyed the instructions of the prophet.

I will never forget how ferociously the water was hitting the rocks. Early in the morning, we threw the salt and stretched out our hands over the water. God was gracious and answered our prayers. The anticipated storm did not hit San Antonio. As we commanded the morning, God baffled the minds of the logicians and statisticians and calmed the storm.

I believe God has given us authority over the elements. Faith without works is dead. Let's use it by speaking to the elements early in the morning. We can do this!

Following is a prayer for commanding the morning. Be sure to pray this out loud. Also, I have included declarations for commanding the morning in the appendix that you can use each day. When you get an understanding of what you're praying, begin to expound with your own words as you read through the prayer. Finally, be prepared to receive prophetic insight from God as you pray, and make a list of the things He speaks to you to use in your prayer time.

THE COMMANDER OF THE MORNING PRAYER

Father God, in the name of Jesus, I rise early to declare Your lordship! I get under the covering and anointing of the early riser. I come in agreement with the heavens to declare Your glory. Lord, release the mysteries to me to bring heaven down to earth. The stars (chief angels) are battling on my behalf ahead of time.

My appointed times have been set by God in the heavens. I declare spermatic words that will make contact with the womb of the morning and make her pregnant. At sunrise the dawn will give birth to the will of God, and light will shine on wickedness to shake it from the heavens. At twilight my enemies will flee, and newly found spoils will await me at my destination. My destiny is inevitable!

O God, let my prayers meet You this morning! I command the morning to open its ears unto me and hear my cry. Let conception take place so that prayer will rain down and be dispatched upon the earth to do Your will.

I command the earth to get in place to receive heavenly instructions on my behalf. My lands are subdued. I command all the elements of creation to take heed and obey the words that are released from my mouth. As my praise resounds and

59

the day breaks, the earth shall yield her increase unto me. I pray out loud and declare that the first light has come.

The firstfruits of the morning are holy, and the entire day will be holy. I prophesy the will of God to the womb of the morning so the dayspring (dawn) will know its place in my days. I decree that the first light will shake wickedness (devised at night) from the four corners of creation. The boundary lines (my portion) have fallen on my behalf in pleasant (sweet and agreeable) places, and I have a godly (secure) heritage. The angels are ascending and descending according to the words that I speak. Whatever I bind or loose on earth is already bound or loosed in heaven. Revelation, healing, deliverance, salvation, peace, joy, relationships, finances, and resources that have been demonically blocked are being loosed unto me now! What is being released unto me is transferring to every person that I associate myself with. I am contagiously blessed!

As I command the morning and capture the day, time is redeemed. The people of God have taken authority over the fourth watch of the day. The spiritual airways and highways are being hijacked for Jesus. The atmosphere of the airways over me, my family, my church, my community, my city, my state, my nation, and the world are producing a new climate. This new climate is constructing a godly stronghold in times of trouble. The thinking of the people will be conducive to the agenda of the kingdom of heaven.

Every demonic agenda or evil thought pattern designed against the agenda of the kingdom of heaven is destroyed at the root, in Jesus' name. I come in agreement with the saints— as we have suffered violence, we take it by force! No longer will we accept anything demonic that is dealt to us. I declare that the kingdom has come and the will of God will be done on earth as it is in heaven.

As the sun rises today, let it shine favorably upon the people and the purposes of God. Daily destiny is my portion. I have no thought for tomorrow. I grab hold of the wings of the morning and ride on the will of God into a new day of victory. God, You separated the night and the day to declare my days, years, and seasons. I am the light of the earth, and I have been separated from darkness. This light declares my destiny.

The Lord has given me dominion over all the elements and all the works of His hands. He has placed them under my feet. Because I fear the name of the Lord, the sun of righteousness shall arise with healing in His wings, and I shall tread down the wicked until they become as ashes under my feet. I commit to walk in this dominion daily. I decree and declare a new day, a new season, and a fresh anointing. As the ordinances of the constellations have received orders from God on my behalf (Job 38:32), they shall manifest in the earth realm. The ingredients of my destiny are programmed into my days, years, and seasons. I bind every force that would attempt to capture my destiny illegitimately.

I plead the blood of Jesus over every principality, power, ruler of darkness, and spiritual wickedness in high places assigned against my purpose. I bind every destiny pirate, destiny thief, and destiny devourer, in the name of Jesus. They are dethroned and dismantled and have no influence over my days. Every curse sent against my days is reversed and boomeranged back to the pits of hell. I displace the Luciferian spirit. I bind every false light bearer and counterfeit son of the morning. My prayer will disrupt dark plans and give my enemies an unprosperous day. I have victory over my enemies every morning. Because I obey the Lord and serve Him, my days will prosper! This is the day that the Lord has made, and I will rejoice and be glad in it. In Jesus' name, amen!

DECLARATIONS FOR COMMANDING THE MORNING

- The heavens declare the glory of God (Ps. 19:1). I too open my mouth and declare God's glory.

- I volunteer "in the day of Your power; in the beauties of holiness, from the womb of the morning" (Ps. 110:3).

- As I command the morning, You cause the dawn to know its place that it might take hold of the ends of the earth, and the wicked will be shaken out of it (Job 38:12–13).

- "To You I have cried out, O Lord, and in the morning my prayer comes before You" (Ps. 88:13).

Note: Every time we rise, we enter into a day that the Lord has made, and we are commanded to rejoice and be glad in it.

- "This is the day that the Lord has made; I will rejoice and be glad in it" (Ps. 118:24).

- I am Your child, and I shall spend my days in prosperity and my years in pleasures (Job 36:11).

- "Let the peoples praise You, O God; let all the peoples praise You. Then the earth shall yield her increase; God, our own God, shall bless us" (Ps. 67:5–6).

- "The lines (inheritance or lot in life) have fallen to me in pleasant (sweet and agreeable) places; yes, I have a good (legitimate and conforming to the established rules that God has laid out for me in the heavens) inheritance" (Ps. 16:6, AMPC).

- The Lord has given me the keys of the kingdom of heaven, and whatever I bind on earth will be bound in heaven, and whatever I loose on earth will be loosed in heaven (Matt. 16:19).

- I am contagiously blessed like Obed-Edom, my house and all that belongs to me (2 Sam. 6:12).

- "The Lord is good, a stronghold in the day of trouble" (Nahum 1:7).

- "Father, Your kingdom come, Your will be done" (Matt. 6:10).

- "If I take the wings of the morning [the pinnacle or highest point of the morning], and dwell in the uttermost parts of the sea, even there Your hand shall lead me, and Your right hand shall hold me" (Ps. 139:9–10).

- The upright shall have dominion over the foolish in the morning (Ps. 49:13–14).

- "I rise before the dawning of the morning, and cry for help; I hope in Your word. My eyes are awake through the night watches, that I may meditate on Your word" (Ps. 119:147–148).

- I am a child of light and of the day (1 Thess. 5:5).

- Lord, You are the light of the world (Matt. 5:14).

- The sun of righteousness (Jesus) shall arise with healing in His wings. I shall trample the wicked; they will be ashes under the soles of my feet (Mal. 4:2–3).

- Lord, You have made me to have dominion over the works of Your hands; You have put all things under my feet (seat of authority) (Ps. 8:6; Josh. 1:3).

- And "from the days of John the Baptist until now the kingdom of heaven suffers violence [attacks], and the violent take it [overcome their enemies] by force" (Matt. 11:12).

Note: In Lucifer's fallen state he was still known as a light bringer, a daystar, and a son of the morning. These are all counterfeits of the real thing. We are genuine, and when we become early risers to command the morning and capture the day, we displace the devil's false light.

- "How you are fallen from heaven, O Lucifer, son of the morning! How you are cut down to the ground, you who weakened the nations!" (Isa. 14:12).

- I reverse the curse as Nehemiah did. O God, turn their reproach on their own heads, and give them as plunder to a land of captivity! (Neh. 4:4).

- For I "do not wrestle against flesh and blood, but against principalities [chief devils], against powers [demonic special agents], against the rulers of the darkness of this age [world deceivers], against spiritual hosts of wickedness in the heavenly places [spirits of degeneration]" (Eph. 6:12).

CHAPTER 6

PRAY OUT LOUD FOR DELIVERANCE

THROUGHOUT MY WALK with God I have celebrated and observed the feasts of the Lord, one of them being Passover. This is the feast that memorialized God's sparing the firstborn of His people when all the firstborn of the Egyptians died. The Word says, "This day shall be a memorial to you, and you shall keep it as a feast to the LORD. Throughout your generations you shall keep it as a feast by an eternal ordinance" (Exod. 12:14, MEV).

This memorial is significant because Pharaoh refused to let God's people go. The Passover marked a season of deliverance that was being held back by demonic forces manifesting through the leader of Egypt. God sent nine plagues—water turning into blood, frogs, lice, flies, pestilence, boils, hail, locusts, and darkness—and Pharaoh still refused to let God's people go.

After this God sent a tenth plague.

As I was writing this chapter, we had just come out of the Passover feast. This Passover observance was like no Passover I'd ever experienced. What made it so different was that a death spirit called COVID-19 was passing by our doors. Passover that year was not just an observance of what happened in biblical times; the media, government, and world had declared that we were facing a virus that could lead to one of the deadliest times ever in America.

I called a fast, and over ten thousand intercessors joined me for a Facebook Live prayer meeting, as we were shut in our homes by government order. Our Scripture reference was Isaiah 26:20, "Come, my people, enter your chambers and shut your doors behind you; hide yourselves for a little while until the [LORD's] wrath is past" (AMPC). The King James Version of that scripture says until the Lord's indignation passes by. The word *indignation* is *za'am* in the Hebrew, and it means "froth at the mouth i.e. (figuratively) fury (especially of God's displeasure with sin):—angry, indignation."[1]

As I was ministering on this subject on Facebook, I asked the participants, "Does God get mad?" To consider the answer, let us take a look at 1 Kings 19:11–13 (KJV):

> And he said, go forth, and stand upon the mount before the Lord. And, behold, the Lord passed by, and a great and strong wind rent the mountains, and brake in pieces the rocks before the Lord; but the Lord was not in the wind: and after the wind an earthquake; but the Lord was not in the earthquake: and after the earthquake a fire; but the Lord was not in the fire: and after the fire a still small voice. And it was so, when Elijah heard it, that he wrapped his face in his mantle, and went out, and stood in the entering of the cave. And, behold, there came a voice unto him, and said, What doest thou here, Elijah?

I chose this particular passage of Scripture because it was clear that God was upset with Elijah's actions. After seeing God humiliate the prophets of Baal on Mount Carmel by raining down fire from heaven while their god was silent, Elijah had the nerve to run for his life when the wicked queen Jezebel threatened to kill him. Elijah ran into the wilderness, sat down under a juniper tree, and prayed for God to take his life.

The Lord responded by sending an angel to give Elijah food, and that food carried the prophet for forty days while he went to Horeb, the mountain of God. That's where God spoke the words we just read. Was God mad? Yes! He told Elijah to anoint Hazael as king over Syria, Jehu as king over Israel, and Elisha as a prophet in his place. Notice what God did there—He replaced an entire administration, including Elijah the prophet.

GOD IS WORTHY OF OUR RESPECT

God is a God of love. He is *agape*! But He had zero tolerance for Elijah's crying, complaining, and finger-pointing when there were seven thousand other prophets who had not bowed their knees to Baal. Putting it simply, the God of Abraham, Isaac, and Jacob is not one to play with. Nahum 1:2–3 says

- God is jealous,

- God avenges,

- God is furious,

- God will take vengeance on His adversaries,

- God reserves His wrath for His enemies,

- God is slow to anger,

- God will not acquit the wicked, and

- God "has His way in the whirlwind and the storms, and the clouds are the dust of His feet" (v. 3).

My using the Scripture is not to preach gloom and doom but to remind us that God is the Creator and we must give Him the respect He is due. Too much disrespect for God has taken place in America. During the COVID-19 pandemic, the United States was given a *selah* moment, a time to pause and think on the things of God. All God wants is the glory (credit) that is due Him, and this is not the season to ignore Him.

COVID-19 is here. People are pointing fingers, but the reality is that we can only point fingers at our individual selves. We can only say, "It's me, God, standing in the need of prayer!" It is time to pray to the God of Israel, who rebukes seas and they dry up. Mountains quake and hills melt at His presence. Nahum 1:6 asks, "Who can stand before His indignation? And who can endure the fierceness of His anger?"

The scripture goes on to say that God is

- awesome,
- terrible,
- fierce, and
- furious—and the rocks are thrown down by Him.

You may have heard Campus Crusade for Christ founder Bill Bright and Youth With a Mission founder Loren Cunningham's teachings on the seven mountains of influence: media, government, education, business/the economy, the family, religion, and arts and entertainment. Those mountains are melting before our very eyes. The things we idolize—from athletics to Hollywood to Wall Street—have been placed on the back burner of life. I'm not saying these things are not important anymore. What I am saying is that people are simply trying to breathe. All of a sudden, breath is more important than all the money in the world.

America needs healing. It is my prayer that our hearts would not be hard like Pharaoh's was. What else has to happen for us to bend our knees as a country? "God overlooked the times of ignorance, but now He commands all men everywhere to repent" (Acts 17:30, MEV).

Repentance sounds like such an easy thing to do, but it gets really difficult for the high and mighty and the intellectually astute. Let's read on:

> While Paul waited for them in Athens, his spirit was provoked within him as he saw that the city was full of idols. Therefore he disputed in the synagogue with the Jews and the devout persons, and in the marketplace daily with those who happened to be there. Then some of the Epicurean and Stoic philosophers encountered him. And some said, "What will this babbler say?" Others said, "He seems to be a proclaimer of foreign gods," because he preached Jesus and the resurrection to them. They took hold of him and led him to the Areopagus, saying, "May we know what this new doctrine is of which you speak? For you are bringing strange things to our ears. Therefore we want to know what these things mean." For all the Athenians and foreigners who lived there spent their time in nothing else, but either telling or hearing something new.
>
> Then Paul stood in the middle of the Areopagus, and said: "Men of Athens, I perceive that in all things you are very religious. For as I passed by and looked up at your objects of worship, I found an altar with this inscription:

TO THE UNKNOWN GOD.
Whom you therefore unknowingly
worship, Him I proclaim to you."
—ACTS 17:16–23, MEV

This passage of Scripture is simple to discern. God is not winking anymore! He is taking the foolish things to confound the wise (1 Cor. 1:27). Those who think they are smarter than God are about to have a rude awakening.

> For the preaching of the cross is to them that perish foolishness; but unto us which are saved it is the power of God. For it is written, I will destroy the wisdom of the wise, and will bring to nothing the understanding of the prudent. Where is the wise? Where is the scribe? Where is the disputer of this world? Hath not God made foolish the wisdom of this world? For after that in the wisdom of God the world by wisdom knew not God, it pleased God by the foolishness of preaching to save them that believe. For the Jews require a sign, and the Greeks seek after wisdom:
>
> But we preach Christ crucified, unto the Jews a stumblingblock, and unto the Greeks foolishness; but unto them which are called, both Jews and Greeks, Christ the power of God, and the wisdom of God. Because the foolishness of God is wiser than men; and the weakness of God is stronger than men. For ye see your calling, brethren, how that not many wise men after the flesh, not many mighty, not many noble, are called: But God hath chosen the foolish things of the world to confound the wise; and God hath chosen the weak things of the world to confound the things which are mighty; and base things of the world, and things which are despised, hath God chosen, yea, and things which are not, to bring to nought things that are.
>
> —1 CORINTHIANS 1:18–28, KJV

God takes pleasure in bringing things down that attempt to be higher than Him. There has always been an argument comparing science to God. This is foolishness! God created science; science did not create God. How could something made be compared to the One who made it?

Another fallacy is the extreme misinterpretation of the separation of church and state. American history shows that every major liberation movement was catapulted from the church. From the America War of Independence to the civil rights movement, the church was key. Paul noted that the Athenians on Mars Hill were very superstitious (religious), but they could not understand and discern the power of God. Today people are easily fascinated by magicians, illusionists, and psychics. The world accepts these things because their roots are not in God. But when a person casts out devils as Jesus did in the Bible and prays in tongues, it is considered strange.

Paul said he noticed the people of Athens were praying to the altar of the unknown god. In other words, they were idolizing things they did not understand. With all the money and intellect we have in the world today, it's hard for men and women to understand with their natural minds wild Rhesus monkeys with herpes turning up in Jacksonville, Florida; two-inch queen killer hornets landing on the West Coast of the United States; food shortages in America; and a virus that killed people worldwide every day.

Though COVID-19 passed over my house and no one died or was even sick, many people don't have the same testimony. My family and church are still on the wall and will continue to pray, but many are letting their guards down as cities reopen. The number of people showing up to pray is declining again, and people are getting lax, but I know in my spirit we can't ease up on taking safety precautions, and we definitely can't ease up on prayer. We must remember that it is in God we live, move, and have our very being, and we must happily seek after Him, even though He is not very far from every one of us (Acts 17:27–28).

I don't know what you're going through as you're reading this chapter. You may not be in the midst of a pandemic but still need Passover deliverance. This is the Passover deliverance prayer we prayed on the first night of the feast. Pray it out loud!

PASSOVER DELIVERANCE PRAYER

Father, this season is not about death but about the deliverance of Your people. We have come to a place in this country and around the world (that You created) where we must happily seek after You. We apply the blood of Jesus over our homes, our doorposts, and our mantels. As we plead the blood we make an emotional appeal to present our argument before the high court of heaven. We petition the heavenly Supreme Court, where there are no appointments or elections but only Your divine authority and absolute will. Father, we call You Shafat, the Lord judge who is judge of all judges.

As the accuser of the brethren dares to present his cases against us day in and day out, we plead our case under the blood covering of Jesus and the unlimited power of Your precious Holy Spirit. God, we will remind You that You are God and we are Your people. We plead our cause and say that there is a cause, and we're not gonna let You go until You bless our souls. We grab the horns of Your altar. On this day we summon Your anointing and cry out for Passover deliverance. We renounce the death spirit and come into agreement with the giver of life.

We spiritually file a petition of writ in the Supreme Court of heaven to overrule and override every earthly judgment against us. Shafat, we call on You to overturn every demonic verdict against America, every demonic verdict against our state, every demonic verdict against our cities, every demonic verdict against our churches, ministries, and homes. You said in Your Word that if we, Your people who are called by Your name, shall humble ourselves, pray, seek Your face, and turn from our wicked ways, then You would hear from heaven, and then You (and only You) would heal our land.

God, we cry out and say that our land needs a miraculous healing. Father, we press like the woman with the issue of blood, and we reach past secular opinions, media, religiosity, and every other anti-miracle spirit. We hold on to the hem of Your garment. We put pressure on the spirit realm like the woman with the alabaster box; we press past the indignantly ignorant, and we offer our firstfruit offering. We give You our best when others see it as a waste. In a time of so much need, we plant a seed of humility, and we give You what others see as very expensive. We press and cry like the Canaanite woman in need of deliverance for her child. Lord, Son of David, have mercy on us and let not our children suffer. A thousand will fall to one side and ten thousand to the other, but every terrible calamity will pass by our children. Trouble will pass by our children and our home and even those who are prodigal. Everything with our last name and in our bloodline will live and not die. God, we humble ourselves and partake of the crumbs from the Master's table. We draw from the salvation (soteria) of God. We thank You for healing, deliverance, protection, peace and solace, joy, and prosperity. God, we grip Your unchanging hand. And when the crowd bids us to be quiet, like the blind man we ask You to have mercy. Like the crippled man at the gate beautiful, we ask You to bring attention to our gates and heal us so we can walk as a people again.

And finally, just as the woman who stayed before the judge would not let him rest, God, we're not going to let You rest. We're not going to let You go until You bless our souls. Daddy God, we meet You at the ford of the Jabbok, where Jacob wrestled with You (Gen. 32:22). We may come out with a limp, but we will not let You go. God, we will remind You that every time Your people cried out in the Book of Judges, You raised up deliverers, and we call forth the deliverers in our season: those with the John the Baptist mantles who would declare that the kingdom of God is at hand, those with the mantle of Daniel who will open windows and pray against those things that are legal but not expedient. Lord, let the words of our mouths and the meditations of our hearts be acceptable in Thy sight. O Lord, You are our strength and our Redeemer.

A PANDEMIC HOUSE BLESSING

Over the years I have authored many books with all kinds of prayers. I believe prayers should be specific and tailor-made. James 4 says that many people have not because they ask not as a result of praying amiss. The word translated "amiss" in verse 3 is *kakōs* in the Greek, and it can mean "evil."[2] In this sense, "evil" prayers are simply prayers that are out of the will of God. Praying what we want to pray can be an evil prayer. When Jesus prayed, He didn't pray what He wanted; He prayed the will of the Father.

In the natural a pandemic is an outbreak of deadly disease over a whole country or throughout the world. This house blessing for the pandemic is divided into three parts:

- a blessing over the house
- a prayer against the spirit of fear in the house
- a prayer against the spirit of the age outside the house

Pray this pandemic house blessing out loud!

Thank You, Jehovah, for the blessings of Obed-Edom upon my house. I decree and declare that the ark of the covenant can abide within the walls of my home. Every person, every place, and everything within the perimeters of my property is anointed. God, I draw a bloodline around my property line, and no curse can penetrate or abide. Lord, as I am faithful in Your house and take care of Your sanctuary, I receive the blessing upon my house and my living room. I confess that everything I have need of is in the house.

My house is a safe place in times of trouble. Protection is in my house. Provision is in my house. Power is in my house. I will rule well in my own house as I am commanded by 1 Timothy 3:4. My children are in subjection with all gravity. I will be faithful to provide for every person, place, or thing that concerns my own house, and the spirit of the infidel is far from me and what is mine (1 Tim. 5:8). *Those in my home will not learn to be idle and wander from one house to another. They will not be tattlers, busybodies, or people who speak things that should not be said* (1 Tim. 5:13). *As for me and my house, we will serve the Lord, and our home will be a safe haven during times of trouble. The anointing of Noah's family to endure the flood that people cannot see coming is upon my house.*

My household receives the warning of the Lord and is moved with the fear of God. My home is the ark that's fully equipped to endure every storm, and my bloodline shall condemn the world and become heirs of righteousness which is by faith. My household will prove that he'd been wrong when the rain comes (Heb. 11:7), *and I speak 1 Peter 4:17 over my own home. For the time is come that the judgment must begin at the house of God. And if judgment begins with us, woe unto those who do not obey the gospel of Jesus Christ. I shut my door and spiritually distance my house:*

I confess that my entire household wears the whole armor of God, and we will stand against the wiles of the devil.

My house is built on the rock (Jesus) and will withstand all trials and storms (Matt. 7:24–27).

The ark of God will remain in my house, and the Lord will bless me and my family for generations (1 Chron. 13:12–14).

When it seems evil to others to serve the Lord, I am choosing this day whom I will serve. As for me and my house, we will serve the Lord (Josh. 24:15).

77

If a house be divided against itself, that house cannot stand. I decree that unity and agreement will abide in my house, and nothing will cause it to fall (Mark 3:24).

My house shall be called of all nations the house of prayer, and I will separate my house from every den of thieves (Mark 11:17).

My family will watch as well as pray. We don't know when the master of the house will return, whether it will be in the evening or at midnight or at the cockcrowing, but we will mantle watch and be ready upon the return of our Lord and Savior Jesus Christ.

I prophesy, decree, and declare that peace and tranquility will be unto my house (Luke 10:5).

And even as Solomon built God's house and then built his own house, I declare and command to be legal in the spirit that I will build my house with words. According to the Bible, the Lord shall preserve my soul, thoughts, and acts. I will not tear it down.

I have been young and will one day be old. And even in my old age God will carry me and deliver me through (Isa. 46:4).

The Lord will keep our hearts with all diligence, for out of it are the issues of life (Prov. 4:23).

The name of the Lord is upon the doorpost of my house. It is a strong tower; my family runs into it, and we are safe (Prov. 18:10).

The word of the Lord is upon the doorpost of my house; every word of God is pure. God is a shield unto my house because we put our trust in Him (Prov. 30:5).

The blood of Jesus is upon the doorpost of my house; every calamity, sickness, and attack of the enemy will pass us by.

No weapon that is formed against us shall prosper, and every tongue that has arisen against my household in judgment God shall condemn. This is the heritage of my household (Isa. 54:17).

The Lord is my refuge and my fortress; my God, in him will I trust (Ps. 91:2).

The angel of the Lord encamps around my house because we fear God. Deliverance is our portion (Ps. 34:7).

God makes peace within the borders of my house (Ps. 147:14).

In Jesus' name, amen.

PRAYER FOR FRONTLINE AND ESSENTIAL WORKERS

The following prayer is dedicated to those who work on the front lines every day and make America the mega-force it is. Although it is an effective prayer for the situation it addresses, it is also a prayer exercise that will build you up as an intercessor. Now let's pray out loud for those on the front lines helping us meet our everyday needs!

Father, we thank You for the essential workers in America and around the world. We release a prayer mantle for those on the front lines, the first to respond in times of crisis. We lift up the individuals working from home, tutors of homeschoolers, and all occupations housed in community residences. We lift up health care workers, critical clinical research development and testing teams, health care providers—*physicians, dentists, psychologists, medical practitioners, nurses, social workers, optometrists, speech pathologists, chiropractors, mental health providers, behavioral care workers, personal care attendants, home health aides, home care workers, diagnostic and therapeutic technicians and technologists, hospital and clinical laboratory personnel, all laboratory technicians, and all hospital accounting, administrative, and engineering personnel.*

We release Your power to agencies that provide plasma and blood products, food service providers, maintenance crews, medical records staff, information and operation technology teams, nutrition experts, sanitation workers, and all medical support staff.

Father, we thank You for those on the front lines of ambulance companies, health care associations, blood banks, medical clinics, community health centers, comprehensive outpatient facilities, and diversionary and residential behavior health care providers.

Thank You, Lord, for those who provide care for the elderly and critical care patients in hospitals and hospice. Protect the support staff and medical workers, home health care staff, assisted-living staff, nursing care facilitators, leaders of group homes, and leaders of other facilities with employees that are at high risk.

God, we thank You for sending Your anointing to the psychiatric wards, the state hospitals, and every other facility where people are receiving care for mental health concerns. Lord, please send medical staff and caretakers with a heart and patience to oversee people who struggle in their thought lives.

God, we lift up the economy of the United States and those who make this great country run. We prophesy integrity, loyalty, honesty, and steadfastness to the cause and plead the blood over everything going on that is unseen. Bless the manufacturers and those who allow us to have materials and supplies that are essential. In the name of Jesus, we lift up those who handle the logistics in the warehouses and manage the operation and distribution to companies in this country. God, anoint the chain of command so everyone involved—from the bottom to the top and from the top to the bottom—will have all they need. God, Your Word says that You will supply all our needs according to Your riches in glory.

Lord, we praise You ahead of time. And we thank You for innovation, witty and creative ideas, and the invention of things never thought of that will meet the needs of critical manufacturing.

We pray for truck drivers, couriers, and those who handle massive workloads for packaging and deliveries. Cover the staff in charge of logistics and dispatching when it is needed. We thank You that they will transport without negative incidents and have safe and prosperous journeys.

Father, we speak blessings over the public health system, the community health workers, and those who analyze and compute public health information to be released to the people.

We ask You for favor over our mortuaries, funeral services, crematories, burial and cemetery operations, and those who supply the materials needed for them to function.

Father, we lift up the law enforcement officials across America. We start by repenting for the innocent blood that has been shed by bad players, yet we stand in the gap for those who risk their lives and serve with right motives. We thank You for Your blessings upon public, private, and volunteer officers who enforce the law with justice and truth. Let there be solidarity and unity among the law enforcement agencies and let them advance what is best for the people. We lift up every sheriff's department, police department, emergency medical department, emergency fire and rescue service, and hazardous material response team. God, bless our first responders.

We speak Your blessings over the air medics, emergency crew, and all teams that provide administration, organization, or security support to them. Thank You for covering the emergency response leadership on the national, state, and local levels. God, anoint them to deal with every disaster, pandemic, terrorist attack, and any other emergency that needs crisis intervention.

Father, we thank You for our food and agriculture system and the essential workers in manufacturing plants, grocery stores, pharmacies, food banks, nurseries, greenhouses, and supply stores. We thank You for the manufacturers and ask You to anoint the United States to produce, reproduce, and distribute food in a manner that would continue to declare our country to be a land of milk and honey.

Father, we plead the blood over our restaurants. God, we lift up all the small businesses. Heal the land of the owners who built their businesses on blood, sweat, and tears. Make a way out of no way. Bring manna from the sky and water out of rocks. Jesus, we believe You will provide for America and countries around the world during every wilderness experience.

Father, remember the farmers and farm workers. Bless agribusiness and its support services. We petition You to send Your anointing to stimulate our economy from on high. Allow our latter rain to be greater than our former, and restore our businesses and workforce to a better state than before the pandemic. Your Word says that a workman is worthy of his hire. Let prosperity come whereby workers will be paid top dollar for the services they render. Father, bless the laborers. Bring increase to our workforce.

Jesus, we thank You for blowing Your ruach (breath of God) on the

- grain and oilseed
- animal and livestock feed
- packaging industry
- distribution sector
- manufacturing sector
- truck delivery and transport shipping industry
- farm and fishery industry.

We lift up the leadership of the labor unions and ask You to appoint those with a heart for You and Your people. Bless our warehouse workers, vendors, port workers, inventory controllers, equipment foremen, block chain managers, postal workers, and all those who do essential jobs that make this country prosperous.

We ask for a special blessing upon those in and over our educational system. Anoint the organizational and administrative structure, along with the teaching platforms, of our public, private, charter, virtual, and home schools and all other avenues used to educate our children.

We send special prayers out for those who work at airports, railways, and city modes of transportation, including

- *comptrollers*
- *drivers and pilots*
- *maintenance personnel*
- *safety and security staff*
- *operations personnel*
- *flight attendants, customer service workers, and administrative staff*
- *management*
- *law enforcement*
- *sanitation crews*
- *food services.*

Finally, Father, we lift up the

- *factories and factory workers*
- *energy and renewable energy workers, companies, and resources*
- *information technology and office technology workers*
- *electricity industry*
- *petroleum industry*
- *steam workers*
- *water and waste operational staff and authorities*

- construction crews, builders, and critical workers for infrastructure and city projects
- financial services industry
- churches, ministries, nonprofits, outreaches, and shelters.

We seal this prayer by declaring that all federal, state, local, tribal, and territorial employees who support mission-essential functions and networks (named or not mentioned) will receive the provision, protection, and power of the Holy Spirit. In Jesus' name we pray, amen!

CHAPTER 7

PRAY OUT LOUD FOR REVIVAL

As I am writing this book, the restrictions set in place at the beginning of the COVID-19 pandemic are just starting to ease up. People had been instructed to remain socially distant for nearly a year, and the isolation has brought all kinds of problems. Anxiety, depression, and loneliness have been at an all-time high.

But I prophesy: "This thing the enemy meant for evil will turn around for the good of the church. Though we had been socially distant, we will be spiritually connected, and that connection will not be limited to our buildings. We are the temple of the Holy Ghost! Church of the living God, unite and be the mighty force to be reckoned with that we are called to be, a boomerang against darkness. The devil will wish the pandemic did not come upon America, because America is the ground from which revival shall spring forth—and it shall flow from the temples of men and women filled with the power of God and connected by the Holy Spirit, not just natural edifices, says the Lord of hosts."

God is pouring out His Spirit on all flesh, just as the prophet declared in Joel 2:28: "And it will be that, afterwards, I will pour out My Spirit on all flesh; then your sons and your daughters will prophesy, your old men will dream dreams, and your young men will see visions" (MEV). As God pours out His Spirit in revival, He will use not only men but also women. They too will pray and evangelize as well as pastor, prophesy, and serve as apostles in the church. It is ludicrous to think men are the only ones God will use, and we must renounce this lie in the name of Jesus.

Paul wrote a letter to the church at Rome commending a woman named Phoebe. He said she was a servant of the church at Cenchrea and encouraged the believers in Rome to "receive her in the Lord, as becometh saints, and that ye assist her in whatsoever business she hath need of you: for she hath been a succourer of many, and of myself also" (Rom. 16:2, KJV).

The Greek word translated "succourer" is *prostatis* and refers to "a woman set over others; a female guardian, protectress, patroness, caring for the affairs of others and aiding them with her resources."[1] It is clear that Phoebe was a leader in the church and Paul was impressed with her. He even received support from her.

God is not calling women to be silent anywhere. He is calling women to stand alongside men and make their voices heard on the earth. What would have happened if the woman at the well had been silent after her encounter with Jesus? (See John 4:1–11.) An entire city of men, women, and children would not have been converted.

A LIFE-CHANGING ENCOUNTER

Let's take a minute to really look at the woman at the well's encounter with Jesus. While the disciples were away at the market, Jesus met a woman at Jacob's Well in Samaria. It was around the sixth hour (noon) when the woman approached the well and Jesus asked her to draw Him a drink. The woman asked Jesus how He could even deal with her because she was a Samaritan and He was a Jew and during that time the two groups did not associate.

Jesus told her that if she understood the gift of God and who was asking her for a drink, she would ask Him for a drink and He would give her living water. The woman responded by pointing out that Jesus had nothing to draw water with and the well was deep. How then could He give her living water? She also asked Him if He was greater than Jacob, who provided the well.

Jesus said whoever drinks of the well of which He spoke would never thirst again because He was speaking of a well whose water would spring up into everlasting life. The woman replied, "Sir, give me this water so that I will thirst no more and never have to come to this well again." Jesus then said, "Go get your husband and bring him to Me."

The woman responded that she did not have a husband, and Jesus told her that she had spoken well, that she had no husband because she'd had five husbands and the one she was currently with was not her husband. The woman then received a revelation and perceived that Jesus was a prophet. Jesus ministered to the woman and said that even though some had worshipped on the mountain they were on and some worshipped in Jerusalem, an hour was coming when mankind would not worship according to either.

Jesus explained that God is a Spirit, and when the hour came, true worshippers would worship God in Spirit and in truth. I want you to know the hour is here now! We do not have to go to a particular mountain—a particular church, ministry, or building—or even to that which represents Jerusalem. Those who really worship God can worship Him from wherever they are. No matter what your culture, race, predicament, or lifestyle, allow God to meet you and fill you with His Spirit so you will never go back to whatever He brought you out of.

The name of the woman at the well was never given, but she became one of the most powerful evangelists in the Bible. She was transformed by her experience with Jesus. When the disciples returned from the market, they were puzzled to find Jesus talking to a woman like her. But the Word of the Lord declares that the woman left her water pot at the well and went into the city to testify. This water pot represented whatever she had been carrying to that same old place, never getting her healing or deliverance. She laid it down at the well, which represented a type of altar.

She asked Jesus about the coming of the Messiah, and He said, "I that speak unto thee am He." The woman ran into the city and told everyone, including the men. "Come see a man, which told me all things that ever I did: Is not this Christ?" This was powerful evangelism. She posed the question and asked them to come and see for themselves. Just as she had to see for herself and I had to see for myself, people have to see Jesus for themselves. This is what real evangelism is about. The woman at the well became an evangelist upon her conversion.

Isn't it funny that God sent a loose woman to witness to men? Because they knew her dirt, after she met Jesus they could bear witness to her deliverance.

When God pours out His Spirit, it will reach all flesh as Joel prophesied—both men and women. Women can preach, prophesy, teach, pastor, lead as apostles—and they can pray out loud! Don't let religious tradition silence the voice of women in the church.

A REVIVAL THAT EMPOWERS EVERYONE

> Let your women keep silent in the churches, for they are not permitted to speak; but they are to be submissive, as the law also says. And if they want to learn something, let them ask their own husbands at home; for it is shameful for women to speak in church. Or did the word of God come originally from you? Or was it you only that it reached?
> —1 CORINTHIANS 14:34–36

This popular passage of Scripture has confused many people when it comes to the topic of women in ministry. When reading these verses, it is important that the time in which they were written and biblical history be strongly considered.

First it should be noted that the church had just received the baptism of the Holy Spirit and started speaking in tongues and walking in the gifts of the Spirit. This was all new. The church was excited, but they were also venturing into things of the Spirit they had never encountered. The second thing to be noted is that at one time women were not allowed to attend church services. When this passage was written, women were coming to church for the first time. Not only did they have to learn about the outpouring of the Holy Spirit; they did not know the simplest things about how to carry themselves in the house of God.

The Spirit of God was moving through His people as had never been seen before. In the Old Testament the Spirit came upon men, but now, as it was prophesied, out of the bellies of God's people was flowing rivers of living water (John 7:38). This move was amazing but demanded order. The people at the church in Corinth needed nurturing when it came to the gifts of the Spirit, especially the wives who were new to attending church. When women were allowed in the sanctuary, the men sat on one side of the room and the women sat on the other. Though the congregation was filled with husbands and wives, they were segregated by gender. It is apparent that the wives were disrupting the service by yelling across the room, asking their husbands questions. This is even clearer when you read 1 Corinthians 14:34–36 in *The Message* (emphasis added):

> Wives must not disrupt worship, talking when they should be listening, asking questions that could more appropriately be asked of their husbands at home. God's Book of the law guides our manners and customs here. Wives have no license to use the time of worship for *unwarranted speaking*. Do you—both women and men—imagine that you're a sacred oracle determining what's right and wrong? Do you think everything revolves around you?

Many people have used this passage to keep women from serving in positions of leadership in the church. But we can't let traditions of men and a spirit of religion shape our theology. Let us stand on the Word of God. Scripture shows us that women were welcomed in the early church and served in every area of fivefold ministry, not only as evangelists, like the woman at the well.

Apostle

In his letter to the Romans, Paul wrote, "Greet Andronicus and Junia, my kinsmen and fellow prisoners, who are noteworthy among the apostles, who also came to Christ before me" (Rom. 16:7, MEV). Paul emphasized that these two were "noteworthy among the apostles." I do not believe this means they were just in the midst of the apostles. I believe they were apostles themselves.

In Romans chapter 16 Paul greeted many believers who ministered with him, but he identified Andronicus and Junia as his fellow prisoners. The Amplified Bible says they were "once" fellow prisoners, which does not appear to point to a spiritual state of bondage but indicates that they were in prison together at one time.

I think it is also important that Paul said these apostles were in Christ before he was. He gave them credit as being his elders. Though some Bible translations changed the name Junia to the male Junias and the matter has been the subject of debate over the centuries, most modern-day scholars believe Junia was a woman.

The Greek word for *apostle* is *apostolos*, which means sent one.[2] The focus of the apostolic anointing should not be the gender of the person but whether he or she is sent by God.

I believe in female apostles—after all, I am a female apostle. But there are some women who have taken on the title of apostle who are not called to the office. We can judge trees by the fruit they bear. You can discern the legitimacy of a female apostle by the fruit of her womb.

- She is a confident woman and is not intimidated. She does not have to fight to prove herself to those of the male gender.

- She has a pied piper anointing, and where she leads many people follow. The apostolic anointing touches more than the few people in a person's circle; it is released throughout cities, to the nation, and even around the world. Though small-group studies are important and apostles can surely lead them, the extent of their ministry does not stop there. The spirit of multiplication is upon the mantle—apostles have an anointing that draws the multitudes.

- She walks in absolute authority. This is when a person has authority in the spirit realm but also has natural authority with supernatural favor. Authority and favor walk hand in hand. The kind of favor that comes with authority is contagious, and it rubs off on the people apostles come in contact with. A woman who walks in absolute authority commands a room with her beauty and valor.

- She is a demon buster, and when she enters a region the principalities are put on notice because the demons know her name. The apostolic anointing draws attention from the dark side, but it also brings increased power over the enemy.

- She has a creative unction called the *prōton* (first) anointing.[3] This causes her to be innovative and do things that have not been done before. She is apostolic in nature, meaning she is the first to do

> many things. Her strategies are hard to duplicate
> because she operates out of the anointing of being
> who God created her to be, which is herself!

Taking on the title of apostle or any other ministerial title that you are not called by God to have can be spiritual suicide. With an apostle mantle comes apostle demons. If you don't have a true mantle for a calling, you will be dealing with unwarranted warfare and will always be under attack. It is important to wait on God and seek Him concerning your high calling.

Prophet

I cannot talk about women prophets without talking about Deborah (Judg. 4). In a culture in which women had no rights, she judged Israel. Deborah sat under a tree, and people from the lowest to the highest rank came to seek her wisdom and guidance. To put it the nicest way I can, she was a bad sister!

One day Deborah summoned the general of the army of Israel, Barak, to come before her. She prophesied the victory of God's army over King Jabin's troops. Barak responded by telling her that he would go to war but not without her. She agreed to go but said it would be at a price. Barak would win, but the glory would go to a woman. That woman was Jael. The Bible declares that she was a "woman of the tent," or a housewife (Judg. 5:24). Jael destroyed General Sisera in her house, and she invited Barak to come and see the spoils (Judg. 4:17–22). A man the army of Israel could not take out was taken down by a housewife.

Deborah was an Old Testament example of a female prophet for sure. The New Testament Scripture says Philip the evangelist had four virgin daughters who were acknowledged as accurate prophets (Acts 21:9). Regarding whether the Bible speaks of female prophets, I close my case!

Pastor

Paul mentioned Euodia and Syntyche in his letter to the church at Philippi (Phil. 4:2–3). He asked them to be on one accord and think the same thing. He also asked others to help them. Paul referred to Euodia and Syntyche as women who had contended together with him in ministry. He also mentioned Nympha (Col. 4:15) and Apphia (Philem. 2) in his letters to the church at Laodicea. He noted that Nympha was having church meetings at her house. (See Colossians 4:15 in the NIV or the Amplified Bible; some versions translate the name as the male Nymphas, interpreting this believer to be a man, but many scholars believe Paul is referring to a female in this text.)[4] With these examples, we can at least acknowledge that women were in leadership during the movement of the New Testament church. They were significant and not silent!

To properly address the position of a pastor in the church, we must define the word *pastor* biblically. The Greek word for pastor is *poimēn*. It means shepherd or one who feeds, protects, and rules over a flock or congregation.[5] *Pastor* is the Latin word for the title. I do not think it is a coincidence that pastors are called shepherds and the congregation is called sheep. A pastor is someone the Lord raises up to take care of the total well-being of His flock and to watch over them.

Psalm 23:4 says, "Yea, though I walk through the valley of the shadow of death, I will fear no evil: for thou art with me; thy rod and thy staff they comfort me" (KJV). Woe unto them who do not understand the power of the rod and the staff of the pastor. The shepherd's rod and staff provide:

- **protection and correction (rod)**—The rod was a short, club-like weapon used to fight off wild animals that got too close to the sheep. The shepherd literally got between the sheep and the wild animals and ran them off with his rod, which is very different from a staff, as the staff was used to pull the sheep back to him, to a safe place.

- **direction (staff)**—Sheep are not survivors, and they cannot hunt for food. Without a shepherd they can wander off into trouble. They easily become vulnerable to predators. This is why pastors are called to maintain a close watch over the members of their congregations. The pastor and his ministerial staff are a great support to members of the church. When the enemy comes in like a flood to cause people to veer away from the Word, stop attending church, or be drawn into adverse lifestyles, the shepherd uses his staff to pull them back in from trouble.

Psalm 23:1 says the Lord is our shepherd. Yes, Jesus is the Chief Shepherd, but in Jeremiah 3:15 God said He will give us shepherds after His own heart who will feed us with knowledge and understanding. In a natural sense sheep are not independent and they easily veer off and are led astray. But when sheep are properly fed, they follow. The main assignment of the shepherd is to feed the flock.

So when they had eaten breakfast, Jesus said to Simon Peter, "Simon, son of John, do you love Me more than these?" He said to Him, "Yes, Lord. You know that I love You." He said to him, "Feed My lambs." He said to him again a second time, "Simon, son of John, do you love Me?" He said to Him, "Yes, Lord. You know that I love You." He said to him, "Tend My sheep." He said to him the third time, "Simon, son of John, do you love Me?" Peter was grieved because He asked him the third time, "Do you love Me?" He said to Him, "Lord, You know everything. You know that I love You." Jesus said to him, "Feed My sheep."

—JOHN 21:15–17, MEV

There is an unspoken message in this passage of Scripture. Jesus was telling Peter that you cannot love Jesus and neglect to love His people. The lesson to be learned is that you cannot properly love God's people without feeding them or giving them the Word of God. A pastor must be able to feed the flock so they will not be easily drawn away by unbiblical doctrines released by ravenous wolves.

Teacher

Acts 18 tells the story of a ministry team named Aquila and Priscilla. The Roman emperor Claudius released an edict that all Jews had to leave Rome, and Paul visited the ministry team after they were put out of the city. The Bible says they met a man named Apollos, who was boldly proclaiming the gospel in the synagogue. He was eloquent, mighty in the Scriptures, fervent in spirit, well versed in the way of the Lord, diligent in speaking and teaching the things of the Lord, and familiar with the baptism of John (vv. 24–28).

When I researched the word *boldly* used in Acts 18:26, I found that it means he was frank in utterance and confident in his demeanor, and his voice waxed bold.[6] In other words, Apollos was speaking the gospel of Jesus Christ out loud in the midst of some who may not have welcomed his message. Although his presentation got people's attention, there was something about it that caused Priscilla and Aquila to pull him to the side.

This ministry team taught Apollos "the way of God more perfectly" (v. 26, KJV). As sharp and prestigious as this man was, he was still lacking. I believe this is a lesson to all who have ears to hear what the Spirit is saying to the church. None of us has arrived. We can all be tutored to a higher level in God. I learned early in the Lord that anything that stops growing is dead. There is always room for growth in God! Apollos had a sharp teaching gift, but iron sharpens iron.

We cannot separate Priscilla from her husband, Aquila. The Word did not refer only to Aquila; he and Priscilla were a team. God used this sister to help this gifted preacher take his ministry to another level. After his encounter with the husband-and-wife team, Apollos "greatly helped those who had believed through grace" (v. 27, MEV).

The body of Christ must understand and respect the anointing of teachers in the church. Teachers have the ability to break down, expound on, and solidly interpret the Word of God. Luke 6:40 says a disciple is never above his teacher, but after training he will be like the teacher. Strong teachers must be trained, released, and reproduced in the church. Just as people are anointed to shepherd, prophesy, win souls through evangelism, and walk in an apostolic anointing, there are those who have a special gift from God to teach His people.

Women be silent? No, speak out loud! Pray out loud! If the woman at the well had been silent, she would have missed her calling. She became a female evangelist after she met Jesus. She left the spirit that she met Jesus with at the well and ran and told the city about Him. And they believed her message because they saw the change in her life.

The Bible clearly gives women license to open their mouths and pray out loud! But since women are the ones who fill up the sanctuaries, I can safely say that if women close their mouths—and their pocketbooks—churches will shut down.

Pray out loud, ladies, and men, please let the women speak.

LET'S PRAY OUT LOUD FOR REVIVAL!

Father, I agree with the winds of revival. A fresh anointing is released upon our families, communities, churches, cities, states, and countries, and the world. In the name of Jesus, the people of God will cast out devils, speak with new tongues, take up serpents, drink deadly things and shall not be hurt, and lay hands on the sick and they shall recover. Revival is in the air conducive to divine recovery. With the authority of my tongue I release revival fire. Agree with the believers that we will

- *recuperate*
- *regain strength*
- *get better*
- *retrieve what was lost*

- *repair the breaches*
- *restore the wells*
- *be rescued*
- *resume our rightful place*
- *be compensated seven times*
- *recruit and evangelize new believers*
- *recapture the power of the movements of old*
- *walk circumspectly and redeem the time*
- *rediscover*
- *retake*
- *bring back*
- *catch up*
- *make good*
- *obtain gain*
- *get reacquainted*
- *reoccupy*
- *replenish*
- *win again*
- *return stronger*
- *come back*
- *pay back*
- *recreate*
- *improve*
- *readjust*
- *reconstruct*
- *reestablish*

- reinstall
- reset.

Not only shall we recover all, but we shall walk in the revival of full recovery all the days of our lives. The lines of the Spirit have fallen upon me in pleasant places (Ps. 16:6), and I stretch out my faith to agree with everyone who believes. I decree out loud that we are in a season of revival that will never cease. Revival winds, revival waves, revival fire—be released!

CHAPTER 8

PRAY OUT LOUD FOR PEACE

IN THE WORLD in which we live, everybody is focused on the next relationship, making money, becoming famous, having the most friends or likes on social media, or getting a new house, car, or other material thing. I know many who have achieved all of this (and more) but lack one life essential: peace!

The definition of *peace* for the purpose of this chapter is to have time that is free from disturbance; tranquility; a season of calm. It can also be defined as a period of rest from war.[1] Most readers of my books have a general working knowledge of warfare and understand what it means to have a lifestyle of doing warfare. I had the privilege of being a staff sergeant in the US Army during Operation Desert Storm. I will never forget how it felt to be faced with real-life war situations. Words are inadequate to describe it. The greatest peace I can remember feeling in my life was when a cease-fire was called and Operation Desert Storm was over. What a peace that really surpasses all understanding!

I believe we need cease-fires to be called in our lives. Though the weapons of our warfare are not carnal, we need rest and recreation. During Operation Desert Storm they would pull soldiers off the front lines and send them to a special place set up in a rear detachment to give them rest and recreation (R&R). Rest and recreation are so important in warfare. You cannot live on the front lines of life's challenges nonstop. There are repercussions to nonstop warfare. The devil is the only being cursed to never get a break. God's people need a break. If you do not take a break from frontline warfare, you will break down. The results of nonstop warfare include nervous breakdowns and anxiety attacks, and the people around you suffer.

God said that for six days we would labor, but on the seventh day we must rest. This is not a suggestion; it is a biblical command. We all need a seventh day to rest and collect ourselves. Exodus 23:12 says, "Six days you shall do your work, and on the seventh day *you shall rest*, that your ox and your donkey may rest, and the son of your female servant and the stranger may be refreshed" (emphasis added). Rest is reserved for the weary; this includes the people you live with, work with, and associate with, and especially those you lead.

Peace and rest are synonymous. You cannot have one without the other. I teach often on the topic of sweet sleep and divine rest. These cannot exist without peace. In Mark 6:31 Jesus told His disciples, "Come with me by yourselves to a quiet place and get some rest" (NIV). Peace is ushered in, in a quiet place. Hebrews 4:9–10 says, "There remains therefore a rest for the people of God. For he who has entered His rest has himself also ceased from his works as God did from His." And Psalm 127:2 says God gives rest to those He loves.

Ecclesiastes 2:22–23 (NIV) sums it up well.

> What do people get for all the toil and anxious striving with which they labor under the sun? All their days their work is grief and pain; even at night their minds do not rest. This too is meaningless.

Ecclesiastes 5:12 declares that "the sleep of a laborer is sweet, whether they eat little or much, but as for the rich, their abundance permits them no sleep" (NIV). This scripture, of course, relates to filthy lucre and the rich who keep the poor impoverished and have no respect for God. But for the believer, Psalm 62:1–2 says, "Truly my soul finds rest in God; my salvation comes from him" (NIV). The psalmist said, "Oh, that I had wings like a dove! For then I would fly away and be at rest" (Ps. 55:6, MEV). When we are weary and heavy-laden, God commands us to go to Him and He will give us rest. This is the inheritance of the saints of God. (See Matthew 11:28–30.)

I know this book is about praying out loud. But the true power in praying out loud comes when we find a refuge, or a quiet place, to get away to for prayer. When children get rowdy or out of order, many parents initiate a practice called time-out. When children are put in time-out, they are put in a place away from the center of everything going on so they can collect themselves.

If you are feeling overwhelmed by the pressures of life, take a time-out. Read the following biblical confessions out loud. Take a deep breath and receive the anointing of the refuge of the Lord through the promises in His Word.

REFUGE (TIME-OUT) CONFESSIONS

- I trust in God at all times; I pour out my heart before him. God is a refuge for me (Ps. 62:8).

- God is my hiding place, my quiet place, and my shield; I hope in His Word (Ps. 119:114).

- God is my refuge and strength and my very present help in times of trouble (Ps. 46:1).

- God has appointed unto me a city of refuge (Josh. 20:2).

- God is my rock, and I trust in Him. He is the horn of my salvation, my high tower, my refuge, and my savior from violence (2 Sam. 22:3).

- When my enemies attempt to oppress me, the Lord is my refuge in times of attacks and trouble (Ps. 9:9).

- I will sing of the Lord and His power, I will sing out loud of His mercy in the morning, for God is my refuge and my defense in the day of war (Ps. 59:16).

- God is my strong refuge (Ps. 71:7).

- God is my refuge and my fortress (Ps. 91:2).

- I looked on my right hand, and there was no man who knew me; refuge failed me because no man cared for my soul. But I cried unto the Lord and declared that He was my refuge and my portion in the land of the living (Ps. 142:4–5).

- In the fear of the Lord I have strong confidence and a place of refuge (Prov. 14:26).

- I shall not make lies my refuge and hide under falsehoods. I renounce every covenant with death, and I come out of agreement with hell. Therefore, when the overflowing scourge comes through, it shall pass by me and all that concerns me. My refuge is in the Lord, and I am safe (Isa. 28:15).

- The Lord is my strength, my fortress, and my refuge in the day of affliction, and the arrows of the heathen shall not penetrate my quiet place (Jer. 16:19).

- I have strong consolation in the Lord. He has provided a safe place of refuge for me and my family, and we lay hold of the hope He has set before us (Heb. 6:18).

If you have suffered from being weary in well doing or you have declared that you just cannot take it anymore—whatever your *it* is—I call a cease-fire and put you into Holy Ghost time-out. It does not matter what your title is or the level of natural or spiritual authority you have—everybody needs R&R.

It is time to recover—and recover all! This chapter is dedicated to praying out loud for peace. But before you can declare peace, you must have peace. You cannot release what you do not have. For every storm in your life, I decree, "Peace, be still!" Be encouraged. You have fought the good fight of faith. Enter into your rest in this lifetime—now, in Jesus' name!

LET'S PRAY OUT LOUD FOR PEACE!

Father God, in the name of Jesus, I receive my inner peace. I declare that every great storm in my life is overcome with great peace. I speak to the root of the wind that is sending every manifestation against my peace; I rebuke the wind that is sending the storm and say, "Peace, be still."

In the name of Jesus, I receive peace—not just any peace but the peace of Jesus Christ; my heart will not be troubled, and I will not be afraid (John 14:27). God has not given me a spirit of fear but of power, love, and a sound mind (2 Tim. 1:7), which is undergirded in peace. I will be careful for nothing, but in everything by prayer and supplication with thanksgiving I will make my petitions known unto God, and the peace of God which passes all understanding shall keep and protect my heart and mind through my Savior, Jesus Christ (Phil. 4:6–7).

I am a peacemaker and not a troublemaker, according to Matthew 5:9. I love life and have seen many good days, and I purpose to refrain from evil. No guile shall come from my tongue. I will avoid evil and do good and seek peace (1 Pet. 3:10–11).

Now the Lord of peace Himself is giving me peace coming from every direction. I will stand in peace. I will lay me down in peace and have sweet sleep and divine rest (Prov. 3:24), and I will wake up in great faith. I will have perfect peace (Isa. 26:3). And I will let the peace of God rule my heart (Phil. 4:6).

I am thankful for the anointing of peace and the power of peace. Mercy, peace, and love are multiplied unto me (Jude 2). I will follow peace with all men, and holiness, because I shall see God's face (Heb. 12:14). I endeavor to keep the unity of the spirit in the bond of peace (Eph. 4:3)—and great peace is my portion. The things I have learned, received, heard, and seen leaders do, I say that. Because I have experienced this, the God of peace shall be with me (Phil. 4:9).

I will be still and know that Jesus is Lord. I will be still and know who God is and that He will be exalted among the heathens, and He will be exalted in the earth realm (Ps. 46:10).

I renounce carnality. I decree and declare that carnality will not kill me, but because I am spiritually minded, life and peace are my portion.

I am a child of the King, an heir of God, joint heir with Christ. Fear has no place in my life because God has not given me a spirit of fear. I am confident that no weapons formed against me shall prosper (Isa. 54:17). Because God is for me, who can be against me? I am more than a conqueror through Him who loves me (Rom. 8:31, 37). Every curse spoken against me is to no avail because I am blessed. Satan cannot curse whom God has blessed. According to Deuteronomy 28, I am blessed coming in and blessed going out. My enemies shall come against me in one way, but God will cause them to flee in seven ways. All that I set my hands to do will prosper. And all the people of the earth shall see that I am called by the Lord. The Lord has made me plenteous in goods. I'm a lender and not a borrower. I am the head and not the tail. I'm above only and not beneath (vv. 3–11).

I am convinced that neither death, nor life, nor angels, nor principalities, nor powers, nor things present, nor things to come, nor height, nor depth, nor any other creature shall be able to separate me from the love of God (Rom. 8:38–39). In Jesus' name, I make this confession and decree and declare it to be so. Amen!

CHAPTER 9

PRAY OUT LOUD FOR JUSTICE

IN A SEASON in America when there are so many injustices, the open abomination of a man being brutally and demonically murdered before our very eyes was a wakeup call. No matter what your political preference, race, denomination, or cultural background, few would disagree that only the devil himself could justify the slaughter of George Floyd.

May 25, 2020, was a sad day in America. Just replace Floyd's face with that of your son, husband, father, or close friend, and it will be easy to have compassion for Floyd and his family. The sad truth is that some will attempt to take advantage of the situation to promote an agenda that in no way relates to the real problem and leaves the root issue unaddressed.

It is no secret that racism and many other injustices remain in our country. Even after the protests, marches, and speeches, the problems still exist. But as long as there is a praying church, there is a solution to the problems of our day. The way to bring healing and justice in our land is to pray out loud!

CLEAN HANDS

The last bill I put into law in the Florida Legislature was a bill awarding money to a man who had been wrongfully incarcerated for forty-three years. There is no amount of money that can replace forty-three years of life spent locked up in a penitentiary, some of them on death row. Despite this, God blessed this man to get some compensation for the wrongful deed done to him.

I learned a lot championing this bill, but the most interesting thing was regarding the issue of clean hands. There were two people involved in the wrongful incarceration case, a nephew and his uncle. The nephew automatically qualified for state-mandated compensation, but the uncle did not qualify because of a clean hands law in Florida. This law stated that even if it was proved that you were wrongfully incarcerated, you could not be compensated if you had been imprisoned for previous crimes. The only way the uncle could be compensated was to have legislation passed in the House of Representatives specifically to award him. So I sponsored a bill.

The uncle was declared to have unclean hands, and I had to give a presentation arguing why the Legislature should override the law and compensate him. To God's glory, my argument prevailed and the uncle was compensated. As a result, this elderly man was given a means to have a more comfortable lifestyle after his release.

The issue of clean hands relates to a biblical principle. James 4:8 says, "Draw near to God, and He will draw near to you. Cleanse your hands, you sinners, and purify your hearts, you double-minded" (MEV). Notice that having clean hands and pure hearts is key in drawing near to God. Psalm 24:3–5 says, "Who may ascend the hill of the Lord? Who may stand in His holy place? He who has clean hands and a pure heart; who has not lifted up his soul unto vanity, nor sworn deceitfully. He will receive the blessing from the Lord, and righteousness from the God of his salvation" (MEV).

As we pray out loud for justice, it is a must that we have clean hands. The opposite of having clean hands is having blood on our hands. In the spirit, dirty hands are hands that have blood on them.

> When I say to the wicked, "You shall surely die," and you do not warn him, nor speak to warn the wicked from his wicked way that he may live, the same wicked man shall die in his iniquity, but his blood I will require at your hand.
>
> —EZEKIEL 3:18, MEV

This scripture shows that our hands can be unclean from sins of commission or omission. In this verse the person had unclean hands because he did not warn the wicked of his wrongdoing. It was a sin of omission. It was not what he did that put blood on his hands but what he did not do. When it comes to having spiritually clean hands, it is all about purification versus contamination. We must be sensitive to the things that will open the doors to spiritual contamination.

> Since we have these promises, beloved, let us cleanse ourselves from all filthiness of the flesh and spirit, perfecting holiness in the fear of God.
>
> —2 CORINTHIANS 7:1, MEV

Just because a person has dirty hands does not mean that individual does not belong to God. David was a man after God's own heart, and he had unclean hands. He had the blood of Bathsheba's husband on his hands after David had him murdered so he could marry Bathsheba. David had the blood of adultery and murder on his hands, but even this did not condemn him because he repented.

Psalm 51 is the proof of David's repentance. In this psalm, David prayed, "According to Your lovingkindness...wash me thoroughly from my iniquity...and cleanse me from my sin.... Create in me a clean heart, O God, and renew a right spirit within me" (vv. 1–2, 10, MEV).

A man after God's own heart is not a man who has done no wrong and is perfect; he is a man who has a heart to *repent!* David did not just mess up; he fessed up. First John 1:9 says that if we confess our sins, God is faithful and just to forgive us and cleanse us from all unrighteousness. Also, John 15:3 says, "You are already clean through the word which I have spoken to you" (MEV). That means we can also be cleansed through the preached, prayed, and prophetic Word of God.

> When you reach out your hands, I will hide My eyes from you; even when you make many prayers, I will not hear. Your hands are full of blood. Wash yourselves, make yourselves clean; put away the evil from your deeds, from before My eyes. Cease to do evil, learn to do good; seek justice, relieve the oppressed; judge the fatherless, plead for the widow. Come now, and let us reason together, says the LORD. Though your sins be as scarlet, they shall be as white as snow; though they be red like crimson, they shall be as wool.
>
> —ISAIAH 1:15–18, MEV

This passage makes it clear that God does not hear the prayers of those with blood on their hands. Believers are quick to quote the scripture that says God does not hear a sinner's prayer, but what about the believer with blood on his or her hands? First

John 3:3 says, "Everyone who has this hope in Him purifies himself, just as He is pure" (MEV).

God is pure. God is clean. God does not hear the prayers of those with unclean hands. It is all about the hands. In 2020, at the beginning of the pandemic, the first thing the authorities told us was to make sure our hands were clean because dirty hands were the easiest way to spread COVID-19. Let me pose this question: What do spiritually unclean hands spread? Our natural minds cannot imagine.

TOUCH NOT THE LORD'S ANOINTED

Keeping our hands clean in the natural prevents deadly diseases, and keeping them clean in the spirit prevents ungodly contamination. These contaminations must be dealt with from an individual, associational, incantational, and generational standpoint.

The blood of Jesus destroys contamination! Hebrews 9:14 says the blood of Jesus purges our consciences from dead works so we can serve the living God. Daniel 12:10 says, "Many shall be purified and made white and tried. But the wicked shall do wickedly, and none of the wicked shall understand, but the wise shall understand" (MEV).

When it comes to having clean hands, we must be wise. One way that I believe people unwittingly contaminate their hands spiritually is by touching God's anointed. This is a very important issue to address because the world we live in has no respect for God's anointed.

Psalm 105:15 says, "Touch not mine anointed, and do my prophets no harm" (KJV). How many people touch God's anointed with their hands in the spirit? How many people disrespect the spirit, gift, and office of the prophet? I know it is common to mock God, His people, and the things of the spirit, but I believe this will be dealt with and people will be put to open shame. We see examples of this throughout Scripture. Consider the following account.

> A man of God came out of Judah to Bethel by the word of the LORD while Jeroboam stood by the altar to burn incense. He cried against the altar by the word of the LORD and said, "O altar, altar, thus says the LORD: 'A child named Josiah will be born in the house of David, and he will sacrifice upon you the priests of the high places who burn incense on you, 'and these men's bones shall be burned upon you.'" He gave a sign the same day, saying, "This is the sign that the LORD has spoken: 'The altar will be torn apart, and the ashes that are upon it will be poured out.'"
>
> When King Jeroboam heard the saying of the man of God who had cried against the altar in Bethel, he reached out his hand from the altar, saying, "Arrest him!" And the hand that he put forth against him dried up so that he could not pull it back in again. The altar also was torn, and the ashes poured out from the altar, just as the man of God had said it would as a sign of the LORD.
>
> The king answered and said to the man of God, "Seek the face of the LORD your God, and pray for me, that my hand will be healed." And the man of God interceded with the LORD, and the king's hand was healed and became as it was before.
>
> —1 KINGS 13:1–6, MEV

This story is the perfect example of touching the anointed of God. The king, who was operating in the authority of his kingdom, stretched his hand toward the prophet to have him seized, and as the king pointed, his arm got stuck in that position. He could not pull his arm back until the prophet petitioned God to restore him.

A person cannot have clean hands if he or she touches God's anointed. In the days we live in, it is common to slander, disrespect, bully, and blatantly hate on God's clergy and ministers. God has allowed it in days past, but I believe He will not wink at this in the days to come. Scripture says heaven and earth will pass away, but His Word won't (Matt. 24:35). If He says touch not My anointed, He means just that.

Many will have to go to men and women of God to beg their pardon so they can pray to get the destroyer off. Who is the destroyer? The spirit of Abaddon. The one who destroys will be released, and people who have no respect for God's chosen ones will suffer until prayers go up on their behalf from the ones they have bullied.

I realize Abaddon is the angel of the abyss mentioned in Revelation 9:11, but it is also the spirit of destruction that will cause the arms of those who touch God's anointed and everything they put their hands to do to dry up and be destroyed if they do not repent and get prayer.

God is calling His people to stand in the gap with clean hands and cry aloud for justice. I have spent more than a decade in government, and there is a place for legislative change. But the only true, lasting change will come when the people of God open their mouths and pray out loud for God to forgive our sin and heal our land, as 2 Chronicles 7:14 says. Let's open our mouths and declare that justice will not be lacking in our nation.

LET'S PRAY OUT LOUD FOR JUSTICE!

The Lord's hand is not shortened at all that it cannot save, nor are His ears dull that He cannot hear. The hands in America that are defiled with blood and the fingers that are defiled with iniquity will be cut off. God, shut the mouths of those who speak lies and the tongues that mutter wickedness. They trust in emptiness, worthlessness, futility, and abominable lies. I bind the works of

- *feet that run to do evil*
- *men who make haste to shed innocent blood*
- *men with thoughts of iniquity*
- *those with desolation and destruction in the paths and highways*
- *those who do not know the way of peace*
- *those who have no justice or right doings in their goings*
- *those who make crooked paths that cause those that go on them to know no peace*
- *things that cause justice to be far from us*
- *those who thwart righteousness and salvation from over-taking us*
- *the evil ones who wait for light but see only darkness*
- *those who walk in false brightness and see only gloom and obscurity*
- *those who grope like the blind, like those with no true vision or clear sight*
- *those who stumble at noonday and twilight*

- *those who live among those full of life but walk around like dead men.*

No longer shall we look for justice and there be none because it is lacking. No longer shall justice be turned away backward and righteousness stand far off. No longer shall truth fall in the city forum. Uprightness will enter into courts of justice.

Father, You declared in Your Word that You sought a man among them that should make up the hedge and stand in the gap before You for the land, that You should not destroy it, but You found none (Ezek. 2:30). We reverse the curse in Jesus' name. There will be intercessors to stand in the gap. Intercessors are coming from the north, south, east, and west!

I call forth

- *commanders of the morning*
- *intercessors on the wall*
- *gap dwellers*
- *those who will make up the hedge*
- *gatekeepers*
- *prayer warriors for every watch.*

God, I decree and declare that just as You would have spared Sodom and Gomorrah if You had found some who were righteous, there will be righteous men and women to stand in the gap for America. I repent on behalf of my nation for the innocent blood shed and the abominations that have been legislated and activated. Have mercy on this country, O God!

Open our eyes so that truth will deliver us. Justice is based on dealing with issues fairly, ethically, and in a sound way guided by truth. Psalm 11:3 warns us that if our foundation is destroyed, the righteous will be left clueless as to what to do. I decree that our foundation is solid, strong, and built on the rock, who is Jesus Christ. Many are the afflictions of the righteous, but we will be delivered from every lier in wait, snare, agenda, and attack against the kingdom. The kingdom of God suffers violence, but we will become the violent in the spirit and take by force that which is our portion. In Jesus' name, amen.

JUSTICE CONFESSIONS

Now is not the time to shrink back in prayer. Declare God's Word on justice out loud!

- I will "learn to do well; seek judgment, relieve the oppressed, judge the fatherless and plead for the widow" (Isa. 1:17, KJV).

- I execute true judgment and show mercy and compassion (Zech. 7:9–10).

- I open my mouth, judge righteously, and plead the cause of the poor and needy (Prov. 31:9).

- I execute judgment and righteousness as the Lord commands, and I deliver the spoil out of the hand of the oppressor. I do no wrong; I do no violence to the stranger, the fatherless, or the widow (Jer. 22:3).

- I rejoice with them that do rejoice and weep with them that weep. I mind not the high things, but condescend to men of low estate. I will not be wise

in my own eyes. I recompense to no man evil.
Instead, I provide things honest in the sight of all
men. As much as it is possible, I live peaceably
with all men (Rom. 12:15–18).

- I do what the Lord has shown me—what is good
  and what He requires of me—which is to do
  justly, to love mercy, and to walk humbly with
  God (Mic. 6:8).

- I open my mouth for those who cannot speak; I
  open my mouth and plead the cause of the poor
  and needy (Prov. 8:9).

- I shall do no unrighteousness in court; I shall
  not respect the person of the poor, nor honor the
  person of the mighty, but in righteousness I will
  judge my neighbor (Lev. 19:15).

- When the righteous walk in integrity, blessed are
  their children after them (Prov. 20:7). I choose to
  walk in integrity, and my children will be blessed.

CHAPTER 10

PRAISE HIM OUT LOUD
FOR THE VICTORY

A RE WE LIVING in a day when people are ashamed of the gospel of Jesus Christ? With all the antichrist agendas in our culture, I think it is important that this question be asked. Romans 1:16 says, "For I am not ashamed of the gospel of Christ. For it is the power of God for salvation to everyone who believes" (MEV). From my experience in the political world, this foundational scripture of Christianity is being challenged every day.

It is time for the redeemed of the Lord to say so—not just to declare that they are the redeemed of the Lord but to declare that they couldn't care less about what other folk think about our dedication and sacrifices to God. It is not popular to be radical for God. My response is, "So!" We cannot be addicted to or need the acceptance of people who do not even acknowledge Jesus as Lord. What would make us even contemplate acceptance from those who have rejected Him?

Jesus said, "If the world hates you, you know that it hated Me before it hated you" (John 15:18, MEV). The greatest hate crime in America is the hate that is released against those who love the Lord and are called according to His purpose.

I am sixty years old as I am writing this book, and I have been serving the Lord for over thirty years. This means I have served the Lord for more than half my life, and I can bear witness that serving Him is far better than not serving Him.

Romans 8:28 says, "And we know that all things work together for good to them that love God, to them that are called according to His purpose" (KJV). This verse clearly states two things:

1. All things work out for the good if we love the Lord.

2. All things work out for those of us who are called according to His purpose and understand it.

The call of God means everything! There is an outright assignment to shut the mouths of those who are called by God. Laws will be put into place and cultures will evolve into allowing things we cannot imagine as believers. Books like mine will one day be forced off the market. Today we must open our mouths to cry aloud and spare not. Write books, evangelize, win souls, and—more than anything—do not leave this life without fulfilling the purpose for which you were born.

The world gives open adoration and praise to the things that make their hearts beat fast. It is time for our hearts to beat fast for the Lord. Nothing makes the heart of a person who loves the Lord beat as fast as praise and worship unto the Lord. It's time for us to lift our voices and praise Him out loud!

PRAISE HIM IN ADVANCE

There is power in praising God even before you see the victory. We see evidence of this all over Scripture. In Judges 1 the

Israelites had to go to war against the Canaanites, and God told them to send the tribe of Judah first into battle. Judah means praise. The Israelites entered the battle with praise, and "the Lord delivered the Canaanites and the Perizzites into their hand" (v. 4).

Then, in 2 Chronicles 20, the Israelites were again facing a great enemy. The multitude coming against them was so great that Jehoshaphat called a fast. The king went before the Lord and said, "We have not strength enough to stand before this great army that is coming against us. And we do not know what we should do, but our eyes are on You" (v. 12, MEV).

God told them, "Do not be afraid nor dismayed because of this great multitude, for the battle is not yours, but God's" (v. 15). The next day when they went to battle, they sent the singers out before the rest of the army.

> And when they began to sing and to praise, the LORD set ambushments against the children of Ammon, Moab, and mount Seir, which were come against Judah; and they were smitten. For the children of Ammon and Moab stood up against the inhabitants of mount Seir, utterly to slay and destroy them: and when they had made an end of the inhabitants of Seir, every one helped to destroy another. And when Judah came toward the watch tower in the wilderness, they looked unto the multitude, and, behold, they were dead bodies fallen to the earth, and none escaped.
> —2 CHRONICLES 20:22–24, KJV

You may have heard the song that tells us to praise Him in advance. That's what this passage is talking about. It was after the people of Israel began to sing and praise the Lord that

God sent ambushes against their enemies. Praise is a powerful weapon in the mouths of God's people. We can't wait until we see the answers to our prayers to praise Him. We can't wait until the enemy is silenced before we worship Him. We need to praise before and during the battle, and we need to keep praising Him when our breakthrough comes. It is time for us to praise out loud.

The Scripture says, "I will bless the LORD at all times: his praise shall continually be in my mouth" (Ps. 34:1, KJV). "All times" means at all times, including right now!

Don't hold back. Look at what the Scripture says in Luke 19:

> As soon as He was approaching [Jerusalem], near the descent of the Mount of Olives, the entire multitude of the disciples [all those who were or claimed to be His followers] began praising God [adoring Him enthusiastically and] joyfully with loud voices for all the miracles and works of power that they had seen, shouting, "Blessed (celebrated, praised) is the King who comes in the name of the LORD! Peace in heaven and glory (majesty, splendor) in the highest [heaven]!"
>
> Some of the Pharisees from the crowd said to Him, "Teacher, rebuke Your disciples [for shouting these Messianic praises]." Jesus replied, "I tell you, if these [people] keep silent, the stones will cry out [in praise]!"
>
> —LUKE 19:37–40, AMP

If you hold back, the rocks will praise Him. Tell the Lord, "I refuse to let a rock out-praise me!" As we close this book, I want to encourage you to hold nothing back. If you have breath in your lungs, open your mouth, pray out loud—and praise the Lord!

LET'S PRAISE HIM OUT LOUD!

Father, I pray for every person whose mouth has been shut to prayer or praise by the enemy. I stand in the gap and make up the hedge and get on the wall on their behalf. Their mouths will be open and their prayer and praise will penetrate every demonic barrier. I decree and declare that they will have no more "lazy" praises but will release crazy praise!

Prophetically decree and declare the revelation of these Greek and Hebrew words with enthusiasm and boldness. I have included a sample prayer to get you started.

- **Courts**—*ḥāṣēr*—refers to an enclosed area surrounded by walls, like one trenched into a valley or village.[1]

- **Praise**—*tᵊhillâ* (or *tehillah*, both from *halal*)—refers to the adoration and thanksgiving that humanity gives to God as well as the character of God that deserves praise.[2]

- **Praise**—*ainesis*—is the literal act of giving praise and thanks as an offering.[3]

- **Praise**—*aineō*—is praise directed to God.[4]

- **Put forth**—*ḥānaṭ*—is to be red, ripened, and ready to be picked and eaten; refers to the process of the fig tree.[5]

- **Lips**—*cheilos*—as a place of praise; as a result of what has been poured in—in abundance it must be poured out.[6]

- **Behold**—ḥāzâ—means to have a dream; insight, revelation, to be mentally able to perceive praise and contemplate it with pleasure. To behold and be able to see or have vision to prophesy.

- **Offering**—*minḥâ*—is the biblical term for a gift, tribute, or presentation in honor of God.[7]

God, I enter into Your gates with thanksgiving, and I enter into Your courts with praise. I praise You from the valley as my praise breaks the barriers and limitations in the earth realm to penetrate the heavens. I release tehillah. I adore You! I worship You with my utmost reverence and adoration. Lord, I release my praise in thanksgiving and offer ainesis unto You as my freewill offering.

Hallelujah! I give You the highest praise. My soul praises You from the depth of everything in me. This is my aineō, Lord; let my praise spearhead the courts of heaven. I present my minḥâ to You. This is my gift—my best I give unto You, the first fruit of my praise. Lord, receive the sacrifice of my lips as I bask in the place of praise, because my offering of praise and worship is ripe and ready to be released into the earth realm to give You all the honor, the glory, and the praise!

I declare that I have a revelation and a vision (for praise) to praise You all the days of my life. Jesus, my generations will forever praise You!

PRAISE CONFESSIONS

- I confess that by Him I offer a sacrifice of praise to God continually that is the fruit of my lips, giving thanks to His name (Heb. 13:15).

- According to Psalm 100,

  — I purpose to make a joyful noise to You, Lord;

  — Lord, I serve You with gladness and come before Your presence with singing;

  — I know that You are God and that You made me—I did not make myself! I am Your child and the sheep of Your pasture;

  — I enter into Your gates with thanksgiving and into Your courts with praise;

  — I purpose to be thankful to You and bless Your name, for You, the Lord, are good; Your mercy is everlasting, and Your truth endures to all generations.

- According to Psalm 150,

  — I will praise Him in the sanctuary;

  — I will praise Him in the firmament of His power;

  — I will praise Him for His mighty acts;

  — I will praise Him for His excellent greatness;

— I will praise Him for the sound of the trumpet;

— I will praise Him with the psaltery and harp;

— I will praise Him with the timbrel and dance;

— I will praise Him with the stringed instruments and organs;

— I will praise Him upon the loud cymbals;

— I will praise Him upon the high-sounding cymbals.

Let everything that has breath—everything that has intellect, a soul, vital signs, and a spirit and can feel the wind and vitality of breath—praise the Lord! Lord, I confess Your Word. Because I am in the land of the living, I need to praise the Lord!

NOTES

INTRODUCTION

1. Blue Letter Bible, s.v. *"siōpaō,"* accessed July 26, 2021, https://www.blueletterbible.org/lexicon/g4623/kjv/tr/0-1/.

2. Blue Letter Bible, s.v. *"yāraš,"* accessed July 26, 2021, https://www.blueletterbible.org/lexicon/h3423/kjv/wlc/0-1/.

CHAPTER 1

1. *Merriam-Webster*, s.v. "narcissus," accessed September 13, 2021, https://www.merriam-webster.com/dictionary/narcissus; Wikipedia, s.v. "Narcissus (mythology)," updated August 12, 2021, https://en.wikipedia.org/wiki/Narcissus_(mythology).

2. Blue Letter Bible, s.v. *"antitassō,"* accessed July 26, 2021, https://www.blueletterbible.org/lexicon/g498/kjv/tr/0-1/.

CHAPTER 2

1. Google Dictionary, s.v. "shift," accessed August 25, 2021, https://www.google.com/search?q=shift+meaning&client=safari&rls=en&ei=opUmYefiKdmUwbkP0_Gt4Aw&oq=shift.

2. *Merriam-Webster*, s.v. "transition," accessed July 26, 2021, https://www.merriam-webster.com/dictionary/transition.

3. Google Dictionary, s.v. "gossip," accessed August 12, 2021, https://www.google.com/search?client=safari&rls=en&q=Gossip+meaning&ie=UTF-8&oe=UTF-8.

4. Blue Letter Bible, s.v. *"exousia,"* accessed July 26, 2021, https://www.blueletterbible.org/lexicon/g1849/kjv/tr/0-1/.

5. Blue Letter Bible, s.v. *"dynamis,"* accessed July 26, 2021, https://www.blueletterbible.org/lexicon/g1411/kjv/tr/0-1/.

6. Blue Letter Bible, s.v. *"charisma,"* accessed July 26, 2021, https://www.blueletterbible.org/lexicon/g5486/kjv/tr/0-1/.

CHAPTER 3

1. Lexico, s.v. "press," accessed June 12, 2021, https://www.lexico.com/en/definition/press.

CHAPTER 5

1. "NOAA's 2006 Atlantic Hurricane Outlooks," NOAA, accessed August 9, 2021, https://www.google.com/search?q=gossip&sxsrf=ALeKk02ghE-ywKsYyhLlHxMqyOSmk3XZtg%

2. N'dea Yancey-Bragg, "From Dennis to Matthew: All the Hurricanes That Hit the U.S. Since 2005," *USA Today*, updated August 25, 2017, https://www.usatoday.com/story/weather/2017/08/24/all-hurricanes-hit-u-s-since-2005/598113001/.

CHAPTER 6

1. Blue Letter Bible, s.v. "*za'am*," accessed June 15, 2021, https://www.blueletterbible.org/lexicon/h2195/kjv/wlc/0-1/.

2. Blue Letter Bible, s.v. "*kakōs*," accessed July 15, 2021, https://www.blueletterbible.org/lexicon/g2560/kjv/tr/0-1/.

CHAPTER 7

1. Blue Letter Bible, s.v. "*prostatis*," accessed June 11, 2021, https://www.blueletterbible.org/lexicon/g4368/kjv/tr/0-1/.

2. Blue Letter Bible, s.v. "apostolos," accessed July 26, 2021, https://www.blueletterbible.org/lexicon/g652/kjv/tr/0-1/.

3. *Merriam-Webster*, s.v. "proton," accessed August 19, 2021, https://www.merriam-webster.com/dictionary/proton.

4. "Who was Nympha in the Bible?" Got Questions Ministries, accessed June 23, 2021, https://www.gotquestions.org/Nympha-in-the-Bible.html.

5. Blue Letter Bible, s.v. "*poimēn*," accessed August 25, 2021, https://www.blueletterbible.org/lexicon/g4166/kjv/tr/0-1/.

6. Blue Letter Bible, s.v. *"parrēsiazomai,"* accessed July 26, 2021, https://www.blueletterbible.org/lexicon/g3955/kjv/tr/0-1/.

CHAPTER 8

1. *Merriam-Webster,* s.v. "peace," accessed June 16, 2021, https://www.merriam-webster.com/dictionary/peace.

CHAPTER 10

1. Blue Letter Bible, s.v. *"ḥāṣēr,"* accessed July 26, 2021, https://www.blueletterbible.org/lexicon/h2691/kjv/wlc/0-1/.
2. Blue Letter Bible, s.v. *"tᵉhillâ,"* accessed July 26, 2021, https://www.blueletterbible.org/lexicon/h8416/kjv/wlc/0-1/.
3. Blue Letter Bible, s.v. *"ainesis,"* accessed August 20, 2021, https://www.blueletterbible.org/lexicon/g133/kjv/tr/0-1/.
4. Blue Letter Bible, s.v. *"aineō,"* accessed August 20, 2021, https://www.blueletterbible.org/lexicon/g134/kjv/tr/0-1/.
5. Blue Letter Bible, s.v. *"ḥānaṭ,"* accessed August 20, 2021, https://www.blueletterbible.org/lexicon/h2590/kjv/wlc/0-1/.
6. Blue Letter Bible, s.v. *"cheilos,"* accessed August 20, 2021, https://www.blueletterbible.org/lexicon/g5491/kjv/tr/0-1/.
7. Blue Letter Bible, s.v. *"minḥâ,"* accessed August 20, 2021, https://www.blueletterbible.org/lexicon/h4503/kjv/wlc/0-1/.